Batsto Village
Jewel of the Pines

Barbara Solem
Photographs by Albert D. Horner

Plexus Publishing, Inc.
Medford, New Jersey

First Printing, 2014

Batsto Village: Jewel of the Pines

Copyright © 2014 by Barbara Solem

Published by: Plexus Publishing, Inc.
143 Old Marlton Pike
Medford, NJ 08055

Library of Congress Cataloging-in-Publication Data

Solem, Barbara, 1947-
  Batsto Village : jewel of the Pines / by Barbara Solem ; photographs by Albert D. Horner.
    pages cm
  Includes bibliographical references and index.
  ISBN 978-1-940091-01-3
  1. Batsto (N.J.)--History. 2. Batsto (N.J.)--Social life and customs. 3. Batsto (N.J.)--Economic conditions. 4. Iron industry and trade--New Jersey--Batsto--History. 5. Glass manufacture--New Jersey--Batsto--History. 6. Batsto (N.J.)--Biography. 7. Villages--New Jersey--Batsto--History. 8. Historic sites--Conservation and restoration--New Jersey--Batsto. 9. Pine Barrens (N.J.)--History, Local. I. Title.
  F144.B25S66 2014
  974.9'84--dc23

                                                        2014030368

Printed and bound in the United States of America.

President and CEO: Thomas H. Hogan, Sr.
Editor-in-Chief and Publisher: John B. Bryans
Production Manager: Norma Neimeister
Book Designer: Kara Jalkowski
Cover Designer: Jackie Crawford
Insert Designer: Lisa Conroy
Proofreader: Beverly Michaels
Indexer: Kathleen Rocheleau

www.plexuspublishing.com

To Budd Wilson,
the person who knows and loves Batsto best
and who graciously shares his knowledge
with anyone who asks

Contents

Photographs and Illustrations

CHAPTER 4

CHAPTER 5

CHAPTER 6

CHAPTER 7

CHAPTER 7 (*cont.*)

A Tour of Batsto Today: Special Section of Photos by Albert D. Horner

CHAPTER 8

CHAPTER 9

CHAPTER 10

Acknowledgments

It takes a village, as the saying goes, and this certainly applies to bringing a book to completion. Once again I have to thank my friend Budd Wilson, noted archaeologist and Pine Barrens historian, for his assistance. Budd, who probably knows more about Batsto than any other living soul, read and commented on the entire manuscript, pointing out inaccuracies while offering valuable suggestions at every stage of the writing process. Budd also generously provided me with many of the old photographs that appear in the book.

Batsto Village: Jewel of the Pines would not have gotten off the ground if not for the gracious cooperation and assistance of Rob Auermuller, Superintendent of Wharton State Forest. Rob and Batsto Village historian John Morsa both generously shared their time and expertise and I am grateful for their support.

A very special thank you to Wes Hughes, Chairman of the Batsto Citizens Committee, and the other volunteers who work so tirelessly to bring the story of Batsto alive for its many visitors. I also want to acknowledge the excellent body of work produced and printed in the *Batsto Citizens Gazette* during the years 1966 to 1996. Without the fine contributions of so many Batsto experts and enthusiasts my book would not have been possible.

I particularly want to recognize the wonderful work of Al Horner, Pine Barrens photographer extraordinaire, whose beautiful images immeasurably enhance the manuscript. Al spent countless hours not only taking and preparing original photographs, but also reproducing and enhancing old photos and illustrations. Thanks also to Berminna Solem, talented artist and loving relative, for once again providing me with beautiful drawings that help to bring the story alive.

I want to thank all the terrific people at Plexus who contributed to the book in important ways, including Norma Neimeister, Kara Jalkowski, Beverly Michaels, Lisa Conroy, and Jacqueline Crawford. And since my editor likes to say that the most important work begins after a book is printed and released, I thank Rob Colding and Deb Kranz in advance for their help and support in making *Batsto Village* a commercial success. Tom Hogan, Sr. has my appreciation and admiration for his commitment to keeping history alive by publishing books such as this one.

Finally, my heartfelt thanks to John B. Bryans, superb editor, dear friend, and the foremost reason I am a three-time published author. Without John's support and belief in me none of my work on the history of the New Jersey Pine Barrens would have seen the light of day. He has skillfully guided me through the editorial process on three manuscripts while making the journey an enjoyable one. Becoming a Plexus author has been one of the best experiences of my life; it is the gift that keeps on giving, and for that I am deeply grateful.

Introduction

Batsto Village, located in the heart of the New Jersey Pine Barrens, is an historic site teeming with early American history. The story of Batsto is the story of how hearty men and women harnessed the natural resources of the region and used them to help build a nation. First used by Native Americans for short visitations, Batsto became an ironworks village in 1765 when Charles Read, a prominent businessman and farmer, and a gentleman involved in all aspects of New Jersey colonial government, built an iron furnace there. Read, who was familiar with the Pine Barrens landscape, knew there were large stores of bog ore on the edges of the streams and rivers. He also knew there were vast stands of pine woods which could be turned into charcoal to fuel the furnace. And there was plentiful water in the streams and rivers to operate the water wheel that powered the furnace bellows.

The village, established 10 years before America declared its independence, was crucial in helping a young colony free itself from the yoke of the mother country. Batsto played an essential role in the Revolutionary War by being a principal arms supplier for the Continental Army. Its shipping landing, located at The Forks on the Little Egg Harbor (now referred to as the Mullica River), less than a mile from the village, was a haven for smugglers and privateers considered so important that a British fleet was sent to wipe it out. Even Benedict Arnold, well known for his betrayal of George Washington, made an appearance.

Eighty years later, when a richer ore and a more efficient fuel in the form of anthracite coal was discovered in Pennsylvania, Batsto's dying iron industry was replaced with a glass works, an industry also dependent on the natural resources of the region. Batsto, now a tourist destination deep in the Pine Barrens of New Jersey, was once a place vital to the burgeoning independence and economy of a new nation.

Today, Batsto is an open-air museum where visitors can travel back in time to experience a bygone era. Nestled near the southern border of Wharton State Forest, the village is surrounded by thousands of acres of dense pine forest. Adding to this natural landscape, meandering, tea-colored streams and rivers course through its thick woodlands. With Batsto's unique ecology and history, we are most fortunate that the state of New Jersey has seen fit to preserve it for the enjoyment and education of all its citizens and, indeed, for posterity.

In the Beginning

Batsto lies within the geologic region known as the Atlantic Coastal Plain. Approximately 100 million years ago this area was covered by oceans that were alternately rising and retreating. With each submergence a new layer of earth was laid down, resulting in more than 15 strata of silts, sands, and clays. Approximately five million years ago the seas receded from the Atlantic Coastal Plain for the last time, leaving the porous and nutrient-leached silica sands and the deeper water-saturated sands that today make-up the huge fresh water aquifers beneath the Pine Barrens.

During the Ice Age, which began about one million years ago, there were sub-arctic conditions in the area of southern New Jersey. This created a prairie, tundra-like environment, a landscape devoid of trees. With the retreat of the last glacier, approximately 10,000 years ago, the plant and animal species that inhabit the area today emerged.

Archeological work done at Batsto from 1957 to 1967 indicates that the site was repeatedly visited by humans during the Archaic (6000 to 1000 BC) and Woodland periods (1000 BC to 1200 AD). Though no archaeological work specific to prehistoric habitation has taken place at Batsto, occasional finds during excavations focusing on its industrial history support this theory. Future archaeological excavation geared specifically to prehistoric study may someday yield more detailed information regarding early usage of this site.

Legend tells us that the Lenni Lenape Indians maintained a summer village on a stream in Pleasant Mills, a neighboring village to Batsto. They called the village Nescochague, and a nearby lake and river still bear this name.

2

The word Batsto is said by some to be of Native American origin, but historians believe that Batsto is a derivative of a Scandinavian word "Badstu" meaning bathing place. In his book, *Heart of the Pines*, John Pearce notes that the area surrounding Batsto was referred to as "Swimming River" as early as 1720. An even more interesting conjecture, and perhaps a more accurate one considering Batsto's location on two rivers at the head of navigation, is its meaning in Norwegian. Batstø, with a slash through the o, translated means "a place of small harbor." To add to the speculation, a small town on the west coast of the Oslo Fjord in Norway, bears this same name. Regardless of the origin, the name stuck and has been attached to this place for as long as its history has been recorded.

EUROPEAN SETTLEMENT

In 1758 John Munrow, a local land speculator, purchased three tracts of land that would later comprise the Batsto plantation from the Council of West Jersey Proprietors. Three years later the land was sold to John Fort who established a lumber-cutting enterprise and sawmill on the site. Unfortunately Fort was unable to make a go of it, and, after just a few years of operation, the property fell into fore-closure and was sold at sheriff sale on May 9, 1764.

Richard Wescoat, owner of a nearby tavern, purchased the prop-erty for £300 and a year later sold a half-interest to Charles Read III, who had been the associate judge presiding at the sheriff sale. In partnership with Wescoat and with backing from four investors, Read quickly built an ironworks on the Batsto property.

Charles Read III, who is often called the Ben Franklin of New Jersey, was born in Philadelphia into a prominent family. His grand-father, Charles Read I, had immigrated to the new world in 1679 from his family's ancestral estate, Trevascan in Cornwall, England. Though on his arrival the elder Read first resided in Burlington City, New Jersey, he subsequently settled in Philadelphia. His son, Charles Read II, became a well-known Philadelphia merchant and shopkeeper and served a one-year term as mayor of the city, from 1726 to 1727.

Trevascan, the ancestral home of Charles Read I
in Cornwall, England (photo by Albert D. Horner)

Charles Read III was educated in Philadelphia as well as England and when he was a young man joined the British Navy. He was sent to Antigua in the West Indies on his first assignment, where he met his wife Alice, the daughter of John Thibou, a wealthy planter. After they married, Alice and Charles returned to America, first residing in Philadelphia and later settling in Burlington City.

Read, who had established a law practice after moving to Burlington, soon became involved in public life, eventually serving in each branch of colonial New Jersey government. He was a long-time member of the Assembly, a onetime Secretary of the Province (making him second in command to the governor), and a judge of the New Jersey Supreme Court, also for a time serving as Chief Justice. He was a Commissioner of Indian Affairs and was involved with the establishment of Brotherton, the only Indian Reservation to be established in New Jersey. He was known to be a close confidant to three Colonial New Jersey Governors: Lewis Morris, Jonathan Belcher, and William Franklin, son of Ben Franklin. To round out his public life he served as commander of the Burlington Militia with the rank of colonel.

Aside from his political career and law practice, Read was involved in the timber industry and operated several sawmills on land that he owned. He also possessed several plantations, one in Springfield Township called Sharon and another near Mt. Holly named Breezy Ridge. He was very interested in innovative farming practices, maintaining copious notes on the farming methods of the day.

Along with his many other enterprises, Read was a land speculator, purchasing and selling over 35,000 acres of land in his lifetime. At some point it came to his attention that large stores of bog ore were accumulating in the swamps, rivers, and streams in the area of Batsto; it seems likely that at the time he purchased his half interest in the property he was well aware of these rich ore beds and their potential to support an ironworks.

After establishing the works at Batsto, Read in quick succession built three other ironworks. He built an iron forge at Atsion, located in what is now Shamong Township, an ironworks at Aetna (originally known as Etna), in what is today known as Medford Lakes, and another at Taunton, in what is now Medford Township.

By 1768, Read had over-extended himself financially and was bankrupt. In an attempt to stay afloat he sold his share of Batsto to several of his partners. Though he managed to keep his other ironworks operating for a time by bringing in new investors, his life continued to spiral out of control. He was experiencing serious health problems and for the better part of a year was bed-ridden. On November 13, 1769, his wife, Alice, passed away at the age of 55, following a long illness.

Facing mounting pressure from his creditors, Read decided to go to Antigua in an attempt to gain some much needed cash by settling his wife's estate. Before leaving the country he sold his shares in Atsion and deeded the Aetna Ironworks to his son Charles Read IV. He turned his remaining assets over to his trustees for assignment.

Not much is known of Read's dealings after his departure, though it was later learned that he had returned to America within the year, opening a small shop in Martinsburg, North Carolina. His new life would be short-lived, however, as he died on December 27, 1774.

At the time of his death no one, including his family and close associates, knew of his whereabouts. It was a sad end for this once prominent man who had made such a significant contribution to early American industry.

Process of Making Bog Iron

The advent of the French and Indian Wars (1754–1763) had created a high demand for iron. With all the natural resources needed to make iron available in abundance in the colonies, capital soon began to flow in to support the expansion of the iron industry.

As Charles Read had been keenly aware, there were large stores of bog ore growing on the edges of the rivers and bogs in the Pine Barrens of southern New Jersey. Bog ore, which is a renewable resource, is formed when iron-rich soils are carried into swamps and bogs by continually flowing streams. By complex processes, water soluble iron salts become oxidized either by exposure to air or by being acted on by certain bacteria. The resulting iron oxide is deposited along the edges of streams and bogs where, mixed with mud, it accumulates and becomes bog ore. Bog ore, originally thought to renew itself every 20 years, takes considerably longer than that to replenish. As a result, many of New Jersey's Pine Barrens ironworks of the 18th and 19th centuries were importing ore from other states by the end of their runs, after their ore beds had become exhausted.

Aside from bog ore, pine wood (which was turned into charcoal) was needed to fuel the iron furnaces. Charcoal was made in pits that resembled an upside-down bowl covered with turf. An eight- or nine-foot pole was set vertically in the ground and eight to 10 cords of pinewood were stacked closely around the pole, then covered with turf and sand. A hole was left open at the top to allow smoke and gas to escape. A collier would light the pit by dropping burning kindling into the apex. The wood would then smolder in a slow controlled burn. After the fire burned out, which took about a week, the collier would wait several days for it to cool before raking out the finished charcoal. For centuries, charcoal was the only fuel available that could produce temperatures high enough to melt iron ore.

Bog ore ledge on the Mullica River (photo by Albert D. Horner)

Bog ore after mining (photo by Albert D. Horner)

Collier at charcoal pit (illustration by Berminna Solem)

Oyster and clam shells (lime) were brought in to be used as a flux, or reducing agent, which assisted with the separating of the impurities (slag) from the molten iron during the smelting process. Water which could be dammed and diverted to operate the water wheel was the fourth component needed to operate an iron furnace.

Iron furnaces of the day were built of stone, brick, and iron. These massive structures, towering over 30' high, resembled a pyramid with its top cut off. The Batsto furnace typically operated 24 hours a day, seven days a week. The fillers or bank men worked ceaselessly carting the carefully weighed out ingredients—bog ore, sea shells, and charcoal—across the trestle bridge to the furnace where it was dumped into a hole in the stack. Though the recipe for making bog iron was closely guarded by most ironmasters, traditionally 2½ tons of bog ore and 180 bushels of charcoal were required to produce one ton of iron.

Below in the furnace chambers, the fires were fanned to very high temperatures by bellows sending strong gusts of air into the stack. As the mixture of ingredients or "charge" moved through the furnace stack it was reduced to a molten mass. The impurities or "slag" floated to

Iron furnace cutaway (photo by Albert D. Horner of a Batsto Museum image)

the top and the bog iron sank to the bottom. When the gutter men tapped the furnace the molten iron flowed out and was guided into roughly drawn trenches in the ground called pigs, so named because the trenches were said to resemble a mother sow suckling her young. When the pig iron cooled and hardened it was taken to the forge for further processing.

At the forge, the brittle pig iron was hammered into more durable iron products like bar iron, tools, horseshoes, and wagon rims. In addition to pig iron, the furnaces in the Pines produced cast-iron products such as stoves, fire backs, kettles, sash weights, water pipes, and, during the war years, military munitions.

SMUGGLING AT THE FORKS

For many years the British attempted to control manufacture and trade in the colonies by enacting laws that restricted what the Americans could produce as well as with whom they could do business. In the British view the colonies existed only to enrich the mother country, therefore any laws passed by the Parliament were

Pig iron (photo by Albert D. Horner)

designed to favor British trade. Britain also had an interest in keeping the colonies dependent on the monarchy for manufactured goods which it could sell to them at inflated prices.

The Iron Act of 1750 was passed by the Parliament of Great Britain as a way to encourage the manufacture of pig iron and iron bars by allowing untaxed importation from the colonies. These raw materials, however, could only be sold to British manufacturers. The Iron Act also prohibited the colonies from producing finished iron products, allowing these goods only to be fashioned in England. The finished iron products had a higher value than did the raw materials, thus this law highly favored British trade.

Other British statutes such as the Navigation Acts (1650 and 1696) also restricted American trade by allowing only British ships to transport imported or exported goods to and from the colonies. The only people allowed to trade with the colonies were British citizens, and commodities such as sugar, tobacco, cotton, and wool produced in the colonies could only be exported to British ports.

These restrictive trade laws irritated the colonists, who soon began to circumvent what they perceived as unfair regulations through smuggling. Most early American merchants who were involved in foreign trade were engaged in this practice to one degree or another, and the custom of smuggling became an intricate part of the colonial economy.

Before 1763 the British were preoccupied with their war with France and other problems at home and did little to enforce the Navigation Acts. But the French and Indian Wars had depleted the British treasury, and it was noticed that America was experiencing an unprecedented era of prosperity. At the time it was costing the British £8000 a year to collect £2000 in import duties. It was estimated that £700,000 of merchandise was being smuggled annually. In 1763, the government of King George III—who had just come to the throne—began to clamp down on the colonists as a way to replenish the British coffers.

With the enforcement of the Navigation Acts, the mother country began to make serious efforts to collect the import taxes owed them. With the added tax burden placed on them by the Stamp Act (1765) and Townsend Acts (1767) the colonists began to rebel, citing "taxation without representation." The colonists were creative in their resistance and utilized a variety of methods, including forging clearance papers, bribery, and mislabeling cargoes. The best method, however, for avoiding the hated taxes was to unload goods at ports not patrolled by the British.

The Forks, located on a remote, navigable river less than a mile from Batsto, was one of the smugglers' best kept secrets. Ships of lighter draft could dock there and unload barrels of sugar, molasses, tea, and coffee. The goods would then be transported overland through the woods to Philadelphia. Countless illegal cargoes were brought up the Little Egg Harbor—later called the Mullica River— and carted by horse and wagon to Philadelphia markets.

All was going well for the smugglers of The Forks until an unidentified spy informed custom agents in Philadelphia of the illicit happenings on the Little Egg Harbor. When the locals learned of the betrayal, a contingent of sailors was dispatched to seize the spy. After being tarred and feathered and placed in stocks for a

The Forks (photo by Albert D. Horner)

few days, the spy was freed and told to "go and sin no more." It's not likely he ever again betrayed his colonial countrymen.

With the colonists outsmarting the British in their efforts to control commerce in the colonies, the cold war between the two adversaries began to heat up.

JOHN COX

In 1770, a Philadelphia merchant and trader named John Cox purchased the Batsto Ironworks for £2350. Charles Thomas, Cox's silent partner in the deal, would hold a one-quarter share of the works until Cox bought him out three years later. Given his involvement in trade, it is likely that Cox was himself involved in the smuggling business and knew of the illegal activities at The Forks. He was a staunch and effective patriot, a member of both the first Committee of Correspondence and the Pennsylvania Council of Safety. By 1774 the latter organization had, for all intents and purposes, become the operating government of the colony as royal officials were expelled.

John Cox (painting by Charles Willson Peale, 1792)

In 1760 John Cox married Esther Bowes, the daughter of Frances Bowes, who was the owner of the Black Creek Forge in Bordentown, New Jersey. With these familial connections, Cox was clearly aware of the lucrative market of the iron trade, especially if the colonies were able to free themselves from the domination of Great Britain.

By 1973 Cox had expanded the products produced by the Batsto Ironworks from pig iron to a wide variety of commercial and household articles. This decision was in clear defiance of the Iron Act of 1750, which banned the production of finished iron products by the ironworks in the colonies. The following advertisement appeared in the *Pennsylvania Journal* on June 7, 1775.

Manufactured at Batsto Furnace: In West-New Jersey, and to be sold either at the works, or by Subscriber, in Philadelphia. A Great variety of iron posts, kettles, Dutch ovens, and oval fish kettles, wither with or without covers, skillets of different sizes, being much lighter, neater and superior in quality to any imported from Great Britain— Pot ash and other large kettles, from 30 to 125 gallons; sugar mill-gudgeons, neatly rounded and polished at the ends: grating bars of different lengths, grist-mill rounds; weights of all sizes, from 7 lb to 56 lb; Fuller plates; open and close stoves of different sizes, rag-wheel irons for sawmills' pestles and mortars; sash weights, and forge hammers of the best quality. Also Batsto Pig Iron as usual, the quality of which is too well known to need any recommendation. John Cox

It appears that John Cox was not alone in his defiance of the Iron Act. By the onset of the Revolution, the American iron industry accounted for one-seventh of the world's output of pig iron, wrought iron, and castings.

Before the Declaration of Independence was signed, Cox had a contract with the Pennsylvania Council of Safety to provide large quantities of cannon balls to the Continental Army. Cox had agreed to make delivery by water, but the British blockade of the Delaware River made that impossible. With this deterrent in place Cox found another solution, as evidenced by his letter dated May 22, 1776, to Owen Biddle, who at the request of the Pennsylvania Council of Safety had procured six wagons and teams for Cox.

Six wagons are now loaded and ready to start, and I expect will be at Cooper's Ferry (Camden) by tomorrow Evening. My manager sent off three loads this morning, and I am in hopes that my Overseer, who is gone in Quest of Teams, will return sometime tomorrow with a sufficient number of wagons to take the remainder of the Committee's Order up in the course of next week. You judged well in sending Teams from Philadelphia, it being almost impossible to procure them here at this season of the year, most of the Farmers being busily engaged in planting, and those, who make carting a business, all employed in transporting goods from hence to Philada., Brunswick and New York. P.S. All the Shot ordered by the Committee are Cast.

As the call for independence reverberated across the American colonies, the Batsto Ironworks turned from peacetime products to weapons of war.

Revolutionary War Years

By 1776 the trade at the Forks had turned from smuggling to privateering. Once again, its location at the head of navigation and its proximity to the weapon producing ironworks at Batsto made it an ideal base for clandestine and illicit activity.

On March 23, 1776, the Continental Congress authorized privateering. A privateer is defined as a ship privately owned and crewed but authorized by a government during wartime to attack and capture enemy vessels. Privateering was a way to mobilize armed ships without having to spend treasury resources or commit naval officers. Privateers operated under sanction of "Letters of Marque," (license) issued by the Congress or the state government. With a Letter of Marque privately owned vessels were authorized to harass or prey on British merchant ships. The Library of Congress lists nearly 1700 Letters of Marque as having been issued by the Continental Congress during the Revolutionary War years.

Privateering was a lucrative business for all involved. Any prizes, including the captured vessel and cargo, would be sold at auction and proceeds divided among the owners, officers, and crew. The risks were great (approximately 50 percent of American privateers commissioned were captured by the British), but the profits could be enormous, and it is estimated that 59,000 crewmen engaged in the practice. Navy seamen made meager wages, but a sailor on a privateering vessel could invest eight weeks and be set for life, possibly netting a thousand dollars out of a single cruise in addition to his wages. Any boat capable of being mounted with a cannon could be turned into a privateer.

The Continental Navy had a total of 64 ships, and during the war they captured 196 enemy ships, whereas privateers captured 2,283. Privateers made an important contribution to the war effort and all types of people including members of Congress, military figures, and businessmen bought interests in one or more privateering ventures. It has been stated by historians that privateering caused more harm to the British effort than did the land battles of the Revolutionary War.

By February 1778 the British were reporting that 733 merchant ships carrying cargoes worth $10 million had been lost or captured. By the end of the war American privateers had taken British cargo valued at about $18 million or just over $302 million in today's dollars. Privateers took some 16,000 prisoners, almost as many as were captured by the Continental Army.

The Forks was a natural haven for smugglers and privateers, and the same was true of Chestnut Neck, a village located 18 miles downriver. With its deep harbor and location only a few miles from open sea, Chestnut Neck was the premier site for privateering on the Jersey coast, and it was not unusual for thirty vessels to be anchored in its harbor at a given time.

By June 1776 official privateers were unloading their booty at George Payne's tavern at Chestnut Neck as well as at the House (tavern) of Richard Wescoat at The Forks. At both taverns, goods and vessels captured by privateers would be auctioned off to the highest bidder. Advertisements in New Jersey, New York, and Philadelphia newspapers would blatantly describe the captured goods and ships, notifying prospective buyers of available merchandise. The following advertisement is an example of the many that regularly appeared.

> To Be SOLD by PUBLIC VENUE. On Monday by the third of January inst. At Col. Wescott's at the Forks of Little Egg Harbor, the Scooner FORTUNE, with her tackle, apparel and furniture, per inventory. Also her CARGO, Consisting of about three hundred barrels of flour, a quantity of Indian corn, and a valuable Negro fellow.

By order of the Court of Admiralty of New Jersey
Joseph Potts, Marshall
Pennsylvania Packet 1/2/1779

Cargoes from captured ships reserved for the Continental Army were stored in large warehouses erected at The Forks prior to being carted overland to Washington's troops. A military post was erected there in 1777 to provide protection for the captured goods. A battalion of infantry and a battery of artillery made up the garrison.

As owner of the Batsto Ironworks and an investor in a number of privateering ventures, John Cox must have kept a close eye on the movements of British ships around the Little Egg Harbor inlet. But Cox was not the only prominent citizen with a great deal to lose if the British decided to attack the ports of the Little Egg Harbor.

BENEDICT ARNOLD, NATHANAEL GREENE, CHARLES PETTIT, AND OTHER IMPORTANT PLAYERS

In 1778, Major General Benedict Arnold—who would be best remembered for his treasonous plot to turn Fort West Point over to the British two years later—was responsible for safeguarding the flow of contraband from Chestnut Neck and The Forks to Philadelphia and Valley Forge. Placed in charge of Philadelphia after the British evacuated the city, Arnold had just prior to this assignment purchased a one-half interest in the cargo of a ship called the *Charming Nancy*. Wanting to move the ship out of Philadelphia to a safer harbor, Arnold sent a pass to the captain allowing the ship to proceed undisturbed by the Continental Army. Subsequently, the *Charming Nancy* was captured by a New Jersey privateer whose captain refused to honor Arnold's pass and took the vessel up the Little Egg Harbor River. Arnold was outraged by this incident and took the matter to court.

Shortly after hearing he had won his case, Arnold learned that the British were about to attack privateer bases at Chestnut Neck and The Forks where the *Charming Nancy* had been sent for safety. Alarmed, he used his authority to commandeer 12 military wagons, already commissioned for other duty, to retrieve the cargo of the *Charming Nancy* and cart the goods to Philadelphia.

Arnold's actions in diverting the military wagons for personal use angered many people, and a committee of the Pennsylvania legislature charged him with using government property for private gain. Brought before a court-martial, Arnold was sentenced to be reprimanded by his commander, George Washington. Washington, erring on the side of leniency, gave Arnold a mild rebuke, but Arnold felt unjustly accused and betrayed. From that point forward his relationship with Washington was strained.

Not long after the incident Arnold persuaded Washington to give him command of West Point, New York. It was here that Arnold achieved infamy by betraying Washington to the British Forces.

Two other major players involved with the Batsto Ironworks and happenings in the Little Egg Harbor Inlet were General Nathanael Greene and Colonel Charles Pettit. During the winter of 1776, Greene was encamped with Washington at Valley Forge. He proved to be an outstanding administrator, and Washington subsequently assigned him the duty of procuring supplies for the Continental Army, a position that in the past had been greatly mishandled.

Greene, who has been rated as second only to George Washington in importance to victory in the Revolutionary War, was skillful, trustworthy, and shrewd and was widely regarded as Washington's most capable officer. At this decisive moment in history, he turned to the Batsto Ironworks for the shot and cannon he needed to arm the colonial troops.

Charles Pettit, Secretary to New Jersey Governor William Franklin for a period of time before Franklin sided with the British, was a boyhood friend of Greene and his closest confidant. Both men would become closely associated with John Cox during the Revolutionary War years and with him would form a syndicate that heavily invested in privateering ventures out of the Little Egg Harbor inlet. Eventually each of these men would also own substantial shares in the Batsto Ironworks.

In 1778 Washington asked Nathanael Greene to become his Quartermaster General, a job very similar to today's chief of staff. In

Benedict Arnold (engraving based on a portrait by John Trumbull)

this job Greene would have no direct authority over troops yet he was continually with his commanding officer, whose orders almost always passed through his hands. Initially reluctant to give up his command of troops, Greene agreed to accept the post if Charles Pettit and John

Cox would be appointed as his assistants. At Washington's request, in March of 1778 Congress named Pettit and Cox as Assistant Quartermaster Generals under the supervision of General Greene. In addition to their duties in the field, Greene and his assistants were responsible for procuring all military provisions. In the two years Greene held this job his department dispensed close to $80 million in supplies.

In 1779, at a time when the three men were in charge of procuring cannon and shot for the army, each would hold a substantial financial interest in Batsto. Greene, recognizing a conflict of interest, attempted to hide his ownership. On April 20, 1779 Pettit wrote to Greene:

> I have agreed for as many shares in Batsto as will now afford you, Col. Cox and myself one sixth each.....the stock of coal being short, Mr. Ball blew the furnace out

Charles Pettit (artist unknown)

immediately on getting possession so that now she is idle, waiting for further stock. The only risk we run seems to be from the enemy and if they should learn we are casting cannon that may be something.

Nathanael Greene (painting by Charles Willson Peale)

This letter clearly shows that the men were profiting from the production and sale of weapons to the army for which they were the chief purchasing agents. Also during this time Greene, Cox, and Pettit were diverting government funds which they used to speculate in the privateering trade. It is possible that this money could be chalked up against commissions, but their actions are highly suspect. Several years later when a congressional inquiry was launched to investigate the money dealings of his department, Greene resigned his commission as Quarter Master General. The resignation was accepted, and only Washington's intervention blocked a further congressional probe into Greene's activity.

Though Nathanael Greene's conduct was certainly disreputable and would today have landed him in jail, he went on to distinguish himself as commander of the Southern Campaign. It is also to his credit that Greene was the only general other than George Washington to serve through all eight years of the American Revolution.

Two local businessmen, Major Richard Wescoat and Lieutenant Colonel Elijah Clark—though not as well-known to history as Benedict Arnold, Nathanael Greene, and Charles Pettit—were critical to the happenings at The Forks and Batsto during the Revolution. Both men were active in many anti-British activities, including the privateer trade. Richard Wescoat, an on-and-off-again part owner of the Batsto lands and the keeper of a local tavern, was serving with Washington's army when it crossed the Delaware on Christmas Eve, 1776. Severely wounded at the battle of Trenton on January 2, 1777, Wescoat spent many months recuperating at his home at The Forks.

Elijah Clark, who fought with Wescoat at the Battle of Trenton, was an early resident of the area. He owned a saw mill at The Forks and would build a mansion there in 1762 that stands to this day. After resigning his military commission, Clark served in the New Jersey Assembly between 1777 and 1778. Both men assisted John Cox with the military defense of the Little Egg Harbor inlet and helped organize the running of the British blockade by smuggling much-needed weaponry and other supplies overland to General Washington, whose troops were floundering in Valley Forge.

BRITISH INVASION

By June 1777 the Batsto Ironworks had become such an important supplier to the Continental Army that Cox was given a military exemption for his ironworkers so as not to impair production. In addition, Cox was authorized to set up a company of 50 men to protect Batsto in the event of a British attack. At the time Batsto was making large amounts of cannon and shot, as well as camp kettles and large pans for evaporating salt water. Salt, widely used to preserve food at the time, was in high demand by the army.

An intelligence report found in the British Archives notes that on February 11, 1776, a spy living in the village reported that the Batsto Ironworks was supplying ammunition to the Continental Army. The spy, who according to legend was living in a house on the western shore of Batsto Lake—now the Nature Center—was said to be keeping a sharp eye on the doings of the ironworks and reporting what he saw to British intelligence. An intelligence report written by William Tyron, a colonial governor who fought for the British, notes:

> Shott supplied by John Cox from Batsto Furnace in New Jersey – sent in four wagons – first load-650, 2nd – 400, 3rd – 1128, 4th –445/2623; Weight – ½ of them 6 and the other 9 powders. Sent to Philadelphia for the ships of armed Privateers fitted from that Port.

The house at Batsto that for years was identified as "the spy house" never housed a British spy during the Revolutionary War, as it has been determined by a restoration architect to have been built long after the war ended, in 1820.

In September 1776 local militia built an earthen fort at Chestnut Neck, named Fort Fox Burrows, to provide protection against any British ships entering the Little Egg Harbor inlet. On June 12, 1777, John Cox and Elijah Clark wrote a letter to the Council of Safety noting that the enemy's ships of war had entered the inlet, seizing two brigs lying off Chestnut Neck and carrying them away. The two men implored the council to quickly send funds for additional fortifications. On September 20, 1777, the General Assembly ordered that Cox and Clark be sent funds to erect cannons at Fort Fox Burrows.

The "Spy House" at Batsto (photo courtesy of Budd Wilson)

On June 13, 1778, Cox wrote to Charles Pettit to say he was going to Chestnut Neck in order to raise a small fortification of 8-10 guns. Though Cox, Wescoat, and Clark, who had supposedly borne the cost of arming the fort, were reimbursed £430 1 s. 3 d., no cannon or other heavy artillery were ever erected at Fort Fox Burrows.

During the summer of 1778 three American privateers captured 22 British vessels, two of which had cargo with a combined value of $500,000. The British government was irate and decided something had to be done about the situation at Chestnut Neck and The Forks.

In the autumn of 1778, New Jersey rebel Governor Livingston sent dispatches to Batsto and Chestnut Neck alerting them that the British had had enough and were sending troops to the Little Egg Harbor inlet to destroy the Batsto Ironworks and to put an end to all privateering activity at Chestnut Neck and The Forks.

On September 30, 1778, a British Expedition under the command of Sir Henry Collins of the Royal Navy left New York Harbor. The fleet numbered 13 ships and 1690 men, 400 of them being ground troops commanded by Captain Patrick Ferguson. Their mission was to find and "clean out the nest of rebel pirates" at Chestnut Neck and to destroy the military storehouses at The Forks as well as the ironworks at Batsto.

Due to inclement weather the British expedition did not reach Chestnut Neck until October 5. Colonial intelligence had learned of the impending attack and a dispatch had been sent to Chestnut Neck warning the local militia to shore up the defense. Meanwhile, General Washington had ordered Count Casimir Pulaski and his legion of 333 men to the garrison of Chestnut Neck to assist local militia in fending off the attack. Having been warned, the town-folk of Chestnut Neck acted quickly and moved much of the seized stores and the smaller vessels up river to The Forks for safe keeping. Meantime, Colonel Thomas Proctor's artillery regiment was sent to The Forks to fortify the small military post situated there.

On October 6, British troops rowed onto the shores of Chestnut Neck and confronted the local militia at Fort Fox Burrows. Out-manned and out-armed, the local militia retreated to the woods to await

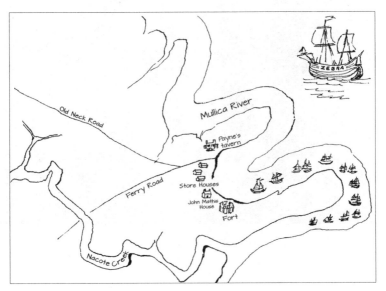

Chestnut Neck (drawing by Berminna Solem based on a sketch by Paul C. Burgess)

Chestnut Neck monument (photo by Albert D. Horner)

The Mullica River at Chestnut Neck (photo by Albert D. Horner)

reinforcements. Unfortunately, Pulaski would not reach the area until October 8. The British raided and burned all of the remaining ships and dwellings at Chestnut Neck. The ships they burned were captured vessels, all of British registry.

On the morning of October 7, Sir Henry Collins, after receiving information that Washington's troops were advancing, decided not to press forward to The Forks and the Batsto Ironworks; at noon the British soldiers and sailors began assembling for withdrawal. On their way out of the area they landed and destroyed three salt works at Bass River.

The British, who were unable to depart the area due to lack of wind, were informed by a deserter of Pulaski's legion that an advance guard of 50 troops were encamped at an outpost near Osborne Island, located on the Great Bay, three miles down river from Chestnut Neck. On October 15, 250 British troops ambushed and massacred 44 of the sleeping soldiers at this outpost. After the attack the British once more attempted a retreat, but several of their vessels ran aground in the inlet. One of these ships, the British flagship *Zebra*, was burned and sunk when efforts failed to refloat it.

Though the Osborne Island massacre was tragic, not one privateer was seized or destroyed during the British raid, and the Batsto
Ironworks, untouched, continued manufacturing weapons for the
Continental Army for the rest of the war. Within a few weeks, the
privateers were back in action on the Little Egg Harbor.

JOSEPH BALL TAKES THE REINS

On October 5, 1778, one day before the British attack on Chestnut
Neck, John Cox sold the Batsto Ironworks to Thomas Mayberry for
£40,000. Six months later, Joseph Ball, who had been manager of
the ironworks under Cox, purchased the property from Mayberry for
£55,000. It would be under Ball's management that Charles Pettit
and Nathanael Greene as well as Cox would purchase substantial
shares in the ironworks.

After selling Batsto, Cox moved with his family to Trenton to live
on an 800-acre estate, originally built by William Trent in 1719. The
estate was located on the Delaware River and Cox would name his
new home Bloomsbury Court; today it is known as the Trent House.
During his four-year residence at Bloomsbury Court, Cox and his
wife, Esther, entertained quite lavishly. Frequent guests included
Generals Washington, Greene, and Knox, Count Rochambeau, and
the Marquis de Lafayette.

John Cox and his wife were interested in finding good matches
for their six daughters and wanted to launch them into the highest
echelon of American society. Thus, in 1791 Cox moved his family
to Philadelphia. He had amassed great wealth from his wartime
activities at Batsto, and during his time in Trenton and Philadelphia
became one of the most influential figures in the political and social
life of the two cities. All the Cox daughters would eventually marry
educated and prominent men.

Joseph Ball was only 32 when he took possession of the ironworks. Credited with the efficient and productive management of
the ironworks during the Revolutionary War years, Ball was born
in Berks County, Pennsylvania, and his early interest in the iron
industry can probably be attributed to his uncle, William Richards,
a previous manager at Batsto and a later owner. Between 1771 and

Joseph Ball (from the historical collection of the Insurance Company of North America)

Trent House, Trenton, Mercer County (photo by Albert D. Horner)

1775 Richards managed the Batsto Ironworks; when he left, Joseph Ball took over as manager.

In 1781 Ball built a forge on the Nescochague Creek, on the site of a former sawmill about one-half mile from Batsto. Prior to the erection of this forge, Batsto was limited to products that could be cast from molten iron. Records indicate that the capacity of the new forge was 200 tons of bar iron per annum. Later, probably in 1783, Ball built a slitting and rolling mill, which turned out sheet iron, nail rods, and rims for wagon wheels, among other products.

During the years Ball was at Batsto, he was one of the principal speculators in the privateering trade of the Little Egg Harbor inlet. It is reported that he made a huge profit from his shares of the captured ships and cargos, which he invested in real estate.

Until the close of the Revolution, Batsto prospered, but with the end of the conflict a post-war deflation set in and commerce declined. The partners' interest in the ironworks also lessened, and in 1784 Ball put Batsto up for sale. He had made important business contacts during the years he was at Batsto and would go on to establish, with Charles Pettit, the Insurance Company of North America. Joseph Ball would eventually become one of the richest men in America.

But Batsto's years of prosperity were hardly over. On July 1, 1784, William Richards purchased the Batsto Ironworks and began a family dynasty that would last 92 years.

Beginning of the
Richards Dynasty

It wasn't unexpected that William Richards (1739–1823), one of Batsto's most effective managers in the course of its industrial history, would one day return to take back the helm. What was unlikely, considering Richards's lack of resources, was that he would one day end up owning Batsto. Even more unlikely, perhaps, was the success he would make of the ironworks, a prosperity that would last into his grandchildren's generation.

Richards, a man who would die wealthy in his mid-80s with an estate valued at more than $200,000, sprang from humble beginnings. The Richards family came to America from Wales in the 1740s and began a hardscrabble life of farming in Eastern Pennsylvania. The life of a colonial farmer was difficult, and the workday was long. The land had to be cleared, the soil plowed, the seeds planted, and the crops harvested. All necessities of life had to be produced by the household, and children contributed greatly to the family's livelihood. It was not uncommon for boys under 10 years old to work by their father's side in the fields and the barns and for young girls to assist their mothers in housekeeping and caring for the younger children. Formal education for the common man was nonexistent in the mid-1700s, and any academic skills acquired by the children came from what their families were able to provide. Though today child labor is considered cruel, it was not unusual for children in colonial America to work 12 hours a day by the time they were 10 years old.

William, a strong and competent boy, enjoyed working beside his father on the farm. But in 1752, when William was just 13, his father passed away, leaving the family in poverty. A year before his death William Sr. had written a will that directed that in the case of his death

William should live with his mother for one year, then be put out to the trade of his choice.

When William was 14 he began an apprenticeship at the Warwick Ironworks not far from his home. An apprenticeship to a skilled craftsmen was a good opportunity for a boy who had few prospects, and William seems to have taken to his new job with enthusiasm. The manager of the ironworks, John Patrick, was apparently so impressed with William that he took him under his wing. The young man formed a close relationship with the Patrick family and was a regular visitor to their home.

William continued to work at the Warwick Ironworks after his apprenticeship was completed. At the age of 25 he married John Patrick's daughter, Mary, 19.

WILLIAM RICHARDS'S DESTINY UNFOLDS

By 1765 the union between the colonies and Great Britain was becoming increasingly strained and dissent was everywhere. One of the last straws for the colonists was the passage by the British Parliament of the Stamp Act. The Stamp Act applied a tax to almost every official document produced in the colonies and, along with the Navigation Acts and Sugar Acts, infuriated the colonists.

Weary of Britain's increasingly heavy yoke, the colonists decided to take matters into their own hands. In Philadelphia, a committee of seven approached the royally chosen stamp distributor and demanded he resign his appointment. Among the committee members was Robert Morris, a wealthy American patriot often referred to as "Financier of the Revolution," who would go on to become a signer of the Declaration of Independence. John Cox and William Richards were also members of this distinguished committee and may have first made one another's acquaintance while participating in this treasonous act.

In 1771 Richards, who had worked at Batsto for a brief period in 1768, returned to serve as its manager under his friend John Cox, who had recently taken possession of the ironworks. When he arrived he brought his family as well as his nephew Joseph Ball, who would later become an owner of the Batsto ironworks.

Richards returned to Pennsylvania in 1775, presumably to serve in Washington's Army. Though he was often referred to as Colonel Richards after the war, there is no record that supports his serving at this rank. A memorandum passed down by the Richards family, however, demonstrates that Richards did serve in some capacity in the continental forces.

After the war Richards returned to Warwick, Pennsylvania, where his family had maintained a residence during the conflict. In January 1781 he received the following letter from Charles Pettit, by then Assistant Quartermaster General and part owner of Batsto.

> Sir:
>
> From the favourable mention Colonel Cox has often made of you as a suitable person.....I have for some time had it in contemplation to make some proposals to you respect-ing the management of Batsto Works, with which you are well acquainted. I have some time ago communicated this intention to Mr. Ball who has other matters in view for himself & therefore cannot long continue in charge of them. He tells me you were lately at the Works and that you intimated a willingness to engage in this Business. Col. Cox and I were together within a few days past, and we have concluded to carry them on with vigor, in order to which we propose to erect a forge as speedily as may be at a place called the Old Mills (formerly Krips Mill), which will make the Works more extensive and conve-nient. If it be convenient for you to engage in the business I should be glad to see you here as soon as possible; not to exceed next week, & if you can come down by Monday or Tuesday I should like it the better, when I imagine I shall be able to offer you terms that may be satisfactory to you. If you cannot come so soon please to let me know by a Line.
>
> CHAS. PETTIT
>
> You will find me the north side of Market Street, next door below 4th Street.

William Richards (portrait by C.B.J.F. de St. Mémin, courtesy of Budd Wilson)

Within a short time of receiving this letter Richards returned to Batsto to serve as its manager. It appears that at least initially his nephew, Joseph Ball, remained at Batsto—probably to oversee his expansive privateering ventures—while continuing to reside in the manor house. This situation proved difficult for Richards who, for the first year, was unable to move his family to the village as proper accommodations were not available. Diary entries by Richards during that first year indicate that he routinely made the 80-mile trip back to Warwick to visit his family, a two-day journey by horseback. After a year Ball returned to Philadelphia, allowing Richards finally to move his wife Mary and their eight children into the Batsto manor house. Three more children would be born to Mary and William while they lived at Batsto.

Batsto prospered under William Richards's management, but as the war drew to an end the price of iron began to drop. The partners, hoping to recoup their investment, offered Batsto for sale on

June 26, 1783. An advertisement describing the ironworks notes, "....a Furnace sufficiently large and commodious to produce upwards of 100 tons of pigs and castings per month." It also lists the presence of a rolling and slitting mill, a forge with four fires and two hammers, a sawmill, a gristmill, and a number of dwellings for the workers. The ad further details the presence of "......a commodious Mansion-House, accommodated with a spacious, well-cultivated garden, in which is a well-chosen collection of excellent Fruit trees of various kinds....." and specified that the river afforded easy navigation for sea vessels of burden within a mile of the village.

With the iron market in decline no buyers appeared. Though Richards had an interest in purchasing Batsto he was unable to come up with the needed cash. After a year with no offers, Pettit, Greene, Cox, Ball, and the other owners, desperate to unload the ironworks, offered Richards a deal. On July 1, 1784 Richards took title of the ironworks while Pettit and Ball continued to each hold a one-third interest. Richards's one-third share, valued at £1,750, was to be paid for with iron he expected to produce in the years to come. As part of the deal Richards was also to be paid £500 annually for managing the ironworks. The ironworks that Ball had purchased in 1779 for £55,000 just five years later was valued at a much reduced £5250.

Richards was an efficient manager, however, and under his direction the ironworks once again prospered. In two years he paid off half of his debt (£980) in iron. By 1790 he had paid off the entire debt and was able to buy out Pettit and Ball, making him sole owner of the ironworks.

Richards managed Batsto like a feudal estate, in much the same manner as iron communities in Pennsylvania where he had done his apprenticeship. He provided everything his workers needed to live and in return he had final say over everything that happened in the village. Workers weren't paid in cash but in scrip that only could be used at the company store. Rare was the worker who did not over-extend his store account, finding his wages used up by the time pay day came around. If a worker needed legal or medical help, his only option was to request it from the big house. Richards was regarded as a fair man who treated his workers well.

Batsto scrip (courtesy of Batsto Village Library)

Although William Richards certainly employed indentured servants, he did not use slave labor at his ironworks as some other New
Jersey works did at the time. He did, however, own two slaves, Andrew
and Ben, who worked in the mansion. Both Andrew and Ben were
given their freedom by decree of Richards's will upon his death in 1823.

Among the many items produced at Batsto during the early years of
Richards's ownership were four firebacks cast for George Washington
in 1787. Two of these firebacks bearing the initials "G.W." and
Washington's family coat of arms can still be seen at Mount Vernon,
one in the west parlor and the other in the master bedroom.

Another interesting Washington connection to Batsto was found in
an ancient ledger, which at one time was in the hands of the King family of Grenloch, New Jersey. It appears that the forebears of a certain
Mrs. King (nee Turner) operated a wagon works and blacksmith shop
in Philadelphia before, during, and after the British occupation. The
ledger in question shows a charge entry for replacing the Washington
coat of arms plaque on the Washington coach, which was noted as
being torn off by a tree limb on the way from Philadelphia to Batsto.
The implication of this ledger entry is that either Washington was at
Batsto himself, or if not, certainly another very important passenger
was. Surely, Washington would have only sent his personal coach on
such a long journey, over poor roads and necessitating an overnight
stay at Batsto, for a high-ranking or prominent associate.

Over the next two decades Batsto continued to prosper and sales
were strong. The products sold during this period were largely pig
iron; bar iron from the forge; six-, seven- and 10-plate stoves; hollow-
ware such as pots, kettles and skillets; sash weights, and other cast-
iron products.

While William Richards clearly made a huge success of Batsto, letters to his son Samuel, who by now was managing the sales of Batsto's
products in Philadelphia, indicate he was not happy living there.
He longed for the company and stimulation that living on a remote
country estate could not offer. To make matters worse, in 1789 he
and Mary lost their three-year-old son Charles, followed in 1793
by their eldest son, John. Six months later their eldest daughter
Abigail passed away. Mary, who had been ill since the birth of her
last child, passed away on February 8, 1794. With the deaths of

his wife and three children within the span of five years, Richards became despondent and continually talked of selling the ironworks. But things were to get even worse for William. In December 1796 he lost his third son, William III, to tuberculosis and three months later his son Joseph succumbed to the same disease. Only six of the eleven children borne to Mary and William were still alive in 1797 and only four would outlive their father.

Three years after Mary's death, the still handsome and vigorous William Richards met a slim young woman from Moorestown, New Jersey, named Margaretta Wood. They married on January 18, 1797, at St. Andrews Episcopal Church in Mt. Holly, New Jersey, a parish where William would hold leadership roles in his later years. At the time of their nuptials, William was 59 and Margaretta thirty-five years his junior at 24. Again Richards found joy in life; the couple went on to have eight children, though three of them would not survive to adulthood.

WILLIAM RICHARDS RETIRES

In 1809 William, who was by then 71, decided it was time to turn the reins of the ironworks over to his 27-year-old son, Jesse.

Stove plates (photo by Barbara Solem, taken at Hopewell Furnace)

Franklin stove (photo by Barbara Solem, taken at Hopewell Furnace)

William had spent 25 years at the helm of the ironworks and felt that Jesse, who had lived most of his life at Batsto, was ready to take over. Along with Margaretta and their four children—two had died in early childhood—William moved to Mt. Holly, where he found the invigorating community he had so missed while living at Batsto. He and Margaretta would have two more children together, the last when he was 77.

Although he no longer managed the day-to-day operations at Batsto, William continued to be active. He kept an eye on the ironworks, which he still owned, while getting involved in other endeavors. He bought and sold real estate and became for a time the Director of the Farmers Bank in Mt. Holly. He held a number of positions in the St. Andrews parish and was also involved in the civic affairs of Mt. Holly.

Aside from Batsto, William owned a large tract of land in Pleasant Mills, seven properties in Mt. Holly, and six properties in Philadelphia, including a tavern. The rents from this real estate as well as the income he received from Batsto made for a very comfortable retirement.

Richards would have one final tragedy in his life when the last son born to him and Margaretta died before reaching the age of 2.

In 1823, William Richards died after having spent 14 years in retirement. He was 85 years old. His will, after providing for the comfort of his wife, directed that the rest of his $200,000 estate be equally divided among his remaining nine children. Richards had already advanced a total of $72,000 to several of his children and this had to be considered as the will was probated. In 1824 the entire estate went up for auction. Most of the Richards properties including Batsto were bought by William's grandson, Thomas S. Richards, the son of Samuel Richards, William's oldest and most successful son.

JESSE RICHARDS TAKES THE HELM

Thomas would retain his Uncle Jesse as manager and five years later would deed him a one-half interest in the ironworks. Five years after Thomas's untimely death in 1839, Jesse purchased Thomas's one-half share for $20,000. In order to make this purchase, however, Jesse was obliged to mortgage the entire Batsto property for $13,425. Though Jesse was finally sole owner of the ironworks, the foreclosure of that mortgage some thirty years later would bring an end to the Richards dynasty.

Jesse Richards, an extremely large man who in later years weighed over 300 pounds, was said to have been "full of enterprise and good nature." He inspired confidence and no one questioned his ability to carry on the family dynasty. At the time he took ownership the ironworks was producing 800 tons of iron each year. During the War of 1812 Batsto supplied munitions for the military. By the time the war ended the ironworks had begun to produce water pipes for the major cities of the East Coast including Philadelphia and Camden. During the 1830s it was estimated that four to six shiploads per week of goods coming and going from Batsto were handled at The Forks landing on the Mullica River.

Jesse Richards (courtesy of the New Jersey State Archives)

In 1837 Jesse launched a schooner called the *Batsto* and later would purchase another vessel, the *Stranger*, for $3000. In 1844 the schooner *Frelinghuysen*, which was built at Batsto, was brought into service. Shipping also occurred in later years from docks at Mordecai Landing, one-quarter mile east of the village, and at Abe Nichol's Landing a bit further down river.

Whereas his father had never been happy at Batsto, Jesse found country living to his liking and would spend the rest of his life there. In 1810 he married Sarah Haskins, the daughter of Rev. Thomas Haskins, an itinerant pastor who often preached at the Batsto/ Pleasant Mills church. The Haskins family had been regular guests in the Richards home, and it was there that Jesse first met his wife when both were children. Sarah and Jesse had seven children together, six of whom lived to adulthood. During his time at Batsto, Jesse became involved in township and county politics and from 1837 to 1839 served as a state assemblyman. He served as Washington Township clerk, as well as on the Burlington County Board of Chosen Free- holders from 1826 to 1845.

During the years Jesse was in charge at Batsto there were at least two sawmills operating, providing lumber, shingles, lath, and other wood products for both construction and shipping. Batsto also made its own bricks during the 1840s and by 1851 was making them by machine.

By the late 1820s the Batsto ore beds had begun to dry up and Jesse began importing iron ore. By the 1830s, the Pennsylvania iron industry was taking off, as a richer ore and a more efficient fuel in the form of anthracite coal had been discovered in the state. In 1838, Jesse, in an attempt to keep up with the rapidly changing industry, installed a "hot blast," a new method of smelting iron. Though he made every effort to keep his ironworks operating, having to ship in ore made it harder for Batsto to compete and gave Pennsylvania iron firms a competitive edge that he could never overcome.

In 1841 Jesse built a cupola furnace. A cupola, or re-smelting furnace, refined pig iron into finished products of a higher quality than had been previously possible. Though Jesse did his best to explore the newest methods of smelting iron, neither the hot blast nor the cupola furnace brought Batsto the prosperity he sought.

Richards mansion (photo courtesy of Budd Wilson)

As the 1840s commenced, less and less iron was being produced at Batsto each year.

But Jesse, with all his challenges, was a determined man who wanted desperately for Batsto to survive. He was quite aware that another industry had taken hold in the New Jersey Pine Barrens and that just down the road in Green Bank a glass plant owned by Nicholas Sooy was producing window panes and bottles. South Jersey had a good source of sands (silica) as well as an abundance of wood for fuel and a nearby supply of lime (seashells), three of the raw materials needed in the production of glass.

In 1845 Jesse formed a partnership with James Brookfield, an expert on glassmaking using the cylinder method. Together, they built a glass plant several miles west of Batsto at New Columbia, now Nesco. A year later, the two built a glass works at Batsto. The partnership between Brookfield and Jesse would be dissolved in 1848, less than three years after it began.

In 1848 the Batsto iron furnace would go out of blast for the last time, though the cupola furnace operated intermittently until 1855. But it was a new day, and window glass would soon bring a revitalized prosperity to Jesse Richards and his beloved Batsto.

The Glass Years

Jesse Richards built the Batsto Glass Works in the field next to the sawmill, behind a row of workers' homes. By 1848 the glass complex consisted of eight structures, a pot house, two melting furnaces, a flattening house, a cutting house, a lime shed, a wood shed, and an oven. An archeological excavation conducted by Budd Wilson in the mid-1960s revealed the location of each of these buildings.

The Batsto glass workers were drawn from other glass plants in southern New Jersey, lured by the advertisement listing free rent and transportation. In the early years, these workers made anywhere from $300 to $500 annually, depending on their skill level and specialty, and were paid in scrip that could only be used at the company store. The scrip system was a tradition that worked well for many years, as

Batsto glassworks (photo courtesy of Budd Wilson)

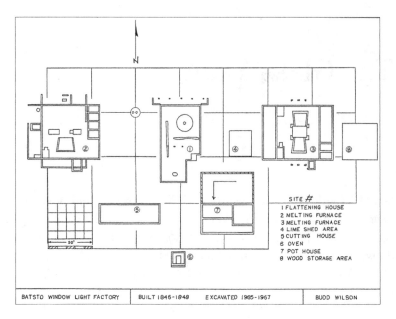

Glassworks diagram (courtesy of Budd Wilson)

the material needs of men working 12-hour days, often seven days a week, were few. There was little time for leisure beyond church activities, and virtually everything a villager needed was available at the company store.

An 1850 census indicates that there were 66 households with a total of 322 people in Batsto. Jesse's household alone consisted of 13 people, which at the time included his wife Sarah, four of his children, his mother-in-law, Sarah Haskins, and six servants. 1850 was a good year for Jesse; his estate was valued at $300,000, and 17,871 100-foot boxes of glass valued at $68,081 were shipped from his docks on the Mullica River to markets up and down the East Coast.

Forty-seven men were employed at the Batsto Glass Works that year. Aside from the glass workers there were many other jobs that required both skilled and unskilled labor. Workmen were needed to chop and haul the wood, wheelwrights to make the wagon wheels, blacksmiths to shoe the horses, ironworkers to smelt the iron, farmers to grow the food, millworkers to grind the grain and saw the logs, carpenters to craft the molds and shipping boxes, brickmakers to mold the bricks, and carters to haul goods to and from the landings. It appeared that Batsto was once more a thriving village.

CASPAR WISTAR

The glass made at Batsto was produced by the cylinder method, also referred to as the "German sheet" or "broad glass" method, introduced into the American colonies in 1739 by Caspar Wistar.

Wistar, a Philadelphia button maker, immigrated to America from the Palatine region in Germany in 1717. One day, while traveling through southern New Jersey selling his buttons, he noticed the abundance of white sand common to the region. He also took note that there was plentiful wood, clay, and water transportation nearby. Wistar was experienced in running a factory using heat, having previously operated two ironworks in Berks County, Pennsylvania, and he immediately recognized the area as an ideal location for a glass plant.

In 1738 Wistar paid the passage for four experienced German glass workers to come to America. With their assistance he established the Wistarburg Glass Manufactory in Alloway, New Jersey. Wistarburg, in operation until 1782, was the first successful glassworks in America.

Prior to the introduction of the cylinder method the only window glass available was the small-paned and more expensive English crown glass. With the introduction of this new method, demand for the more economical window glass, referred to as "lights," grew quickly. By the 1840s South Jersey glass had gained a national reputation for its quality. Jesse Richards was well aware of this, and he also knew that two of the raw materials needed to make glass, namely sand and wood, were readily available on his property.

ROBERT STEWART

On December 1, 1846, Robert Stewart, a man whose destiny would be entwined with Batsto for decades to come, began work as Jesse Richards's bookkeeper. He was paid a salary of $600 a year and was given a rent-free house as well as a 20 percent discount at the company store.

Robert Stewart had been born in Ireland in 1803. He was educated in mathematics and, before moving to America, had worked as a schoolmaster. He came to America with his wife, Margaret, in 1839 and pursued a career in accounting. For a time he worked as a bookkeeper for the Philadelphia-owned firm Hayes and Son's Glassworks in Winslow, New Jersey. But Stewart was unhappy with the accommodations at Hayes, and when Jesse offered him the bookkeeper position at Batsto he jumped at the opportunity. He would become a valuable and trusted employee, and as the years progressed was given increasing responsibility.

The Stewart family was financially secure, having come to America with substantial funds. Stewart was collecting rents from property he owned in Ireland, and his wife Margaret was a person of her own means. When Jesse, who had become a good friend, experienced a financial setback, Stewart not only loaned him $5000 but relinquished his salary for a period of time. It was a gentleman's agreement, a matter between trusted friends, and no paperwork was drawn up to record the transaction. It was just a temporary setback, after all, and surely Jesse Richards, a man known for his integrity, was a man who would make good on his debts. There would be more unsecured loans to Richards in the years to come and long intervals without pay, sacrifices the Stewart family would later bitterly regret.

PROCESS OF MAKING GLASS

Silica (sand), lime (sea shells or limestone), and soda ash (sodium carbonate) are the primary ingredients needed to make glass. In the South Jersey factories, pine wood was harvested to fuel the ovens and melting furnace, which consumed six cords of wood every 24 hours.

Sand and wood were plentiful on the Richards property but the lime and soda ash needed to be shipped in.

The sand was heated in a calcining oven and burned for five to six hours to eliminate moisture and organic matter. The resulting product, after cooling, was sifted through a fine mesh. The wood was thoroughly dried in wood arches located within the melting furnace before being used as fuel. Crushed shells and limestone were also burned in a calcining kiln before being mixed with the other ingredients.

Pots that could withstand the extreme temperature of the furnace without exploding were made by hand in the pot house. The potter's materials included raw clay, burnt clay, and pieces of broken pots. The potter would grind up the materials and carefully sift them before blending them together in a large trough. He would then shape the pots by hand using a mold. Pots were 30" high, up to 2" thick and 2' wide. To ensure slow drying, the pots were cured for six months before being used.

The raw materials (batch), which included the cooked sand, lime, and soda ash, would be put into the handmade pots, which were placed inside the furnace through openings in the furnace called ring holes. It took about 24 hours to turn the batch into molten glass.

Glassblowers or their assistants (referred to as tenders) worked with long hollow blow pipes five feet in length and weighing about 30 pounds. When the glass blower approached the hot furnace he wore a wooden mask with covered eye holes to protect his face from the extreme heat of the furnace. He, or the tender, would gather the molten glass onto the end of the blow pipe from the ring holes. (These holes were closed off during the heating of the batch.) The molten gob of glass gathered by the glassblowers weighed between 50 and 70 pounds.

After gathering the gob of molten glass the glassblower forced it into a hollowed-out block to be formed. This was done several times using increasingly larger blocks until the blower had a sufficient amount of molten glass, referred to as "metal," to form a cylinder.

The glassblower would then mount a perch and blow into his pipe while swinging it over a narrow trapezoidal pit in the floor of the melting furnace, known as the swing pit, until a bubble was

Glassblower or tender (drawing by Berminna Solem)

formed inside the cylinder. The glass blower would continue to swing the blow pipe over the swing pit while forcing air into the pipe until the bubble had expanded and the cylinder reached its desired length and thickness. The finished cylinder would resemble a huge hollow glass bottle 4' to 5' in length. The pipe and cylinder were so heavy that glass blowers would chain themselves to the wall so as not to fall into the swing pit which contained hot, broken glass shards.

Once the cylinder was formed it would be removed from the blow pipe and cut open at both ends. Next it was taken to the flattening house where it was reheated, split, and flattened into sheets of glass 32" by 40".

After cooling, the flattened sheets were carried to the cutting house where they were cut into individual window lights, or panes. The glass cutters, who were considered highly skilled, had to make sure they were cutting the glass into exact sizes without waste. After cutting the window lights, workers packed the glass into wooden boxes with straw separating the layers.

Glassblower with blow pipe (photo courtesy of Budd Wilson)

Inspecting the glass cylinders (photo courtesy of Budd Wilson)

The sizes of the glass varied from 6" by 8" to 26" by 36". Boxes were made to hold either 50 sheets of lights (half box) or 100 sheets (full box). Aside from window glass, the Batsto Glass Works also made the trapezoidal-shaped panes used in municipal street lights.

Batsto glass was marketed according to the quality of the glass. There were four grades: 1st quality was called "Union Extra," 2nd was "Union First," 3rd was "Greenbush Patent," and 4th was "Neponset Patent." The window lights were later marketed in only two qualities, "Washington" and "Sterling."

In the period from 1846 to 1847, 6511 boxes of window lights were shipped from Batsto to the markets of Philadelphia, New York, and other large cities on the East Coast. In 1850 and 1851, when two furnaces were in operation, 19,550 boxes of glass were shipped annually. In the years 1854 to 1867, when only one glass plant was in operation, lesser amounts of glass were sold.

During the years 1846–1854 glass was shipped from the docks on the Mullica River. From 1854 to 1866 the glass was carted by horse and wagon to Weymouth Station (now Elwood) to be shipped by the Camden and Atlantic Railroad and, after 1861, to the Atsion Station once the Delaware Bay and Raritan Railroad had begun operation. A planned railroad that would have traversed the village never materialized, adding to the transportation difficulties faced by the works. In 1867, the last year of glass production at Batsto, the window lights were once again shipped via the Mullica River on the steamboat *Eureka*.

PROBLEMS BEGIN TO APPEAR

Though glass production brought new life to Batsto Village, it also led to numerous problems. The first glass factory was destroyed by fire on April 23, 1847. Although it was rebuilt, months passed without production, causing major losses for the works. The second glass factory burned down in January 1850 and, though it was also rebuilt, this created further delays in manufacture. In 1851 there was further trouble when incoming complaints revealed deficiencies in the glass. The middle men reported that a large percentage of window lights had been poorly packed, had broken corners, were blown too thin, and were not uniform in quality.

But Batsto was dealt its most critical blow with the death of Jesse Richards on June 17, 1854. Jesse had not been in good health for a number of years and had been depending on his son Thomas to handle much of his correspondence. His weight, along with his penchant for alcohol, almost certainly contributed to his health issues. During the last years of his life, in an effort to improve his well-being, he made numerous visits to the Mansion of Health, a grand hotel located on Long Beach Island in what today is Surf City, New Jersey. The Batsto record books report that after a particularly serious illness, Jesse took a tour of the mountains of Pennsylvania to improve his health.

Jesse left his estate, estimated at $100,000, to his wife Sarah, three daughters, Elizabeth, Anna Maria, and Sarah, and three sons, Thomas, Samuel, and Jesse. Thomas, who was a graduate of Princeton University, would carry on the business for his family. Like his father, Thomas served as a member of the New Jersey Assembly and for a time was a state senator. He was also involved in Burlington

Jesse Richards's tombstone (photo by Albert D. Horner)

County and Washington Township politics. Thomas was cultured and likable but was not prepared for the life of managing an industrial village, a fact that would quickly become evident.

With iron sales all but nonexistent, Thomas chose to focus on lumber and glass but after Jesse's death only one glass plant operated. Trouble continued to plague Batsto and on June 13, 1856, a fire once again closed down the plant. For well over a year the glassworks did not operate, largely due to a national recession that reduced demand. The glassworks reopened in the fall of 1857 and remained in steady operation through 1860, other than during the few summer months.

In 1859 the notation "J. Buckeleau hands" begins to appear on the Batsto records. The circumstances are unclear, but it seems likely that a man named Buckeleau was either hired as a manager or was providing the workers for the glassworks. In 1860 the ledger notations change to "Buckeleau and Holmes hands." In 1861 Buckeleau's name disappears and Holmes's appears regularly.

In the fall of 1860 Thomas turned the full operation of Batsto over to Robert Stewart, though he continued to live in the mansion. A fire halted operations for three months in 1861. In 1862 through 1863, possibly due to the industrial prosperity surrounding the Civil War, the glassworks operated almost full time until another fire shut it down for an extended period of time. In May of 1866 the plant caught on fire again and the glassworks was once more rebuilt, albeit for the last time.

1867 was to bring even more problems. The workers went on strike demanding to be paid in cash instead of scrip. Notations in the Batsto records state, "...the boys refused to work on account of not receiving cash." It appears that the glass workers were no longer willing to accept the old ways of doing business.

During this period the office in New York, run by Thomas Richards's friend Francis Holmes, seems to have been consigned all of Batsto's glass. It appears that because of Richards's debts Holmes acquired control of the glassworks. The loss of large sums through this agency plunged the glassworks into greater financial difficulty. On May 1, 1867, the Batsto records state, "F. H. Holmes took possession of glass works." Batsto shipped its last boxes of glass to New York on June 15, 1867. The fires of the glassworks would not be turned on again. On October 31, 1867, the Batsto ledgers state, "F. H. Holmes came to the works and took away all moveable property from the glass house."

Though the glassworks was out of business, the Richards family still owned a significant amount of property. In an attempt to remain financially solvent, Thomas Richards sold large tracts to the Batsto Farm and Agricultural Company, a real estate group formed for the purpose of subdividing and selling off the Batsto lands as 10- and 20-acre farm plots. An advertisement listing the property for $10 an acre and mentioning the Mullica River and nearby Camden and Atlantic Railroad failed, however, to lure buyers. The planned community never materialized.

Debts continued to mount and lawsuits were brought against the Richards for unpaid bills. Though Robert Stewart was granted a court judgment of $20,000 he was never paid back the money he had loaned the estate. A letter written in the 1860s by his wife Margaret tells the sad story.

In the first place we let Mr. Richards (Jesse) Sr. have $500 in gold at 6%. Robert's salary was $600 and then $700 for a longer time to the war when it was raised to $1200....

We also raised a number of cattle every year which was sold to Mr. Richards but never paid for. Also we got some money from home (Ireland) and that was used to maintain the family. All our earnings the Richards got... and at the end left us without one cent.....

After the work was stopped entirely Robert was offered situations elsewhere but Mr. Richards would not hear of him going. They gave him four promise notes and have left us here quite destitute while they live in luxury and keep a houseful of servants, and all the rum they want to drink.

So now, after the labor of a steady, industrious family for 22 years, here we are, without one foot of ground or one dollar.

The mills remained idle, the store closed, the post office was moved and the buildings began to crumble. With no opportunities available at Batsto, the younger villagers moved away, looking for work. The older ones hung on, doing what they could to survive. In season they picked blueberries and cranberries, in other months they hunted, chopped wood, and gathered sphagnum moss and pinecones for local florists and nurseries. Batsto was soon in the hands of a receiver.

On February 23, 1874, a spark from Robert Stewart's fireplace set his house on fire. The fire quickly spread to other houses in the village. The following unsigned letter to the editor offers an eye-witness account as it appeared in the Feb 28, 1874, issue of the *South Jersey Republican.*

> The inhabitants of the unpretentious village of Batsto, Burlington County, have just been visited with a most distressing calamity.
>
> About twenty minutes before noon, on Monday, the 23d inst., a fire broke out in the residence of Mr. Robert Stewart, that, in two hours, reduced four fifths of the most valuable portion of the village to a mass of smoldering ruins. Eighteen of the best houses in Batsto were thus made the prey of the devouring element, and nine families rendered homeless, all of whom lost more or less in household goods and clothing.
>
> The violence of the wind, which at the time, was blowing a gale from the southwest, and the inflammable material of the buildings rendered futile all efforts to save anything within the line of the conflagration. So rapidly indeed did the flames spread, that in forty minutes, half of the buildings in the place were on fire; and the excited occupants were making frantic efforts to save their effects.
>
> The loss, in the aggregate, will probably not exceed ten thousand dollars—that on personal property is from fifteen to eighteen hundred.

After a list of the losses for each family affected, which ranged from $75 to $300, and a description of the path of the fire through the village, the letter continues.

> The origin of the fire is unknown, but is supposed to have been a spark from Mr. Stewart's chimney. The family were in the house not dreaming of danger, when a neighbor rushed up to the gate, calling to them that their house was on fire. The flames had not gained much headway when discovered, but with the furious gale to fan it and the dry hot shingles of the roof to feed upon, it seems to bid defiance to all human efforts to arrest it in its devouring course. In less than ten minutes the air was filled with burning fragments.
>
> The work of removing the goods had been commenced as soon as the fire was discovered, but so rapid was the advance of the flames that before the work in the second story was half done, the stairway was on fire, and Miss Lizzie Stewart was obliged to save herself by leaping from the second story window to the ground, a distance of some ten or twelve feet. Fortunately she sustained no injury beyond a slight sprain.
>
> All was hustle and confusion in the streets. A few of the women seemed to have lost presence of mind and stood wringing their hands in despair; but by far the larger portion—all honor to them—were working as bravely as their husbands or brothers, and much more cooly.
>
> The scene by this time was one of terrific beauty and grandeur—a livid sheet of flame leaping from house to house covered a space of some three acres, and seeming with its intense heat, to lick up the very sand in the street. The surface of the pond was almost blackened with cinders, and far away on the other side, could be seen vast volumes of smoke, where the falling sparks had caught the dry leaves and the line of fire was sweeping off to leeward with the spree of a race horse.

Probably the most stubborn fight of the day was experienced in breaking the line of fire on Water St. The roof of the house occupied by Mr. Brewer was on fire in spots from end to end; but after an hour's sharp work the fire was extinguished and the house saved, though minus a good part of the roof.

As soon as the danger was passed, an active search for empty houses commenced and by night most of the homeless ones who were fortunate enough to save their goods had them in the neighborhood. A subscription was also started immediately, which at this writing amounts to some $300 for the relief of those who had suffered most severely.

As soon as the alarm reached Pleasant Mills, half a mile distant, the factory was closed and all hands sent immediately to render whatever assistance was in their power.

Too much praise cannot be bestowed upon the parties who have acted with such admirable promptness, both in giving their service during the fire, and relieving the suffering after it.

Two years after the fire, foreclosure proceedings began on the 1845 mortgage taken by Jesse Richards. Though there were other judgments, the $13,475 foreclosure took precedence over all other claims. In 1876 Joseph Wharton, Philadelphia financier and industrialist, bought the entire Batsto estate including 36,000 acres, for the price of Jesse's mortgage. Wharton also paid off an excess of $19,000 in liens against the property.

In its 21 years of operation, from September 6, 1846, to June 15, 1867, the Batsto Glass Works produced 229,471 boxes of window lights for cities, businesses, and residences up and down the East Coast. Once again, this tiny village deep within the pine forests of southern New Jersey had made a vital contribution to American life and industry.

Village Life

It was a hardscrabble life for the men, women, and children who lived and made their livelihood at Batsto Village. Life in a company town, where the owner controlled every aspect of the villagers' lives, was never easy, regardless of the product being produced.

Batsto was not an anomaly as regards its system of management. At their peak during the 19th century there were more than 2500 company towns in the United States, housing close to 3 percent of the national population. Company towns were generally built around large production factories and were often established by extractive

Village street (photo courtesy of Budd Wilson)

industries like coal and metal mines. Hershey Chocolate and Corning Glass are two well-known corporations that originally operated as company towns.

A company town resembled a feudal European community. Workers typically lived in isolated settings within minutes of their work, labored long hours with little if any time for leisure, and were paid in scrip that could only be used at the company store. Owners were paternalistic, acting like father figures in providing everything from housing, schools, and churches to law and order and healthcare. The workers and their families had no choice but to obtain everything they needed at the company store, to which they were most often indebted by the time payday came around. These were isolated and self-sufficient communities that depended on the success or failure of the base industry, the productivity of the workers, and the benevolence of the owners.

As we have already seen, there was little time allotted for leisure in these company towns, though 19th-century diaries indicate that men spent considerable time in the local taverns. Church was another

Batsto company store (photo courtesy of the New Jersey State Archives)

outlet for the villagers, who packed the pews when well-known itinerant preachers like the Reverend Charles Pitman preached at the little chapel in Pleasant Mills.

THE WORKERS

The Batsto Iron Furnace operated 24 hours a day seven days a week when the furnace was in blast, generally seven to nine months each year. The furnace would shut down when the pond froze and the water wheel could no longer turn. The men worked one of two shifts, the morning shift that began at 6 am and ended at 6 pm, or the evening one that started at 6 pm and ended at 6 am. The work was often dangerous and grueling, and there was no such thing as paid time off for sickness or vacation. Nor was there a federal protection agency like today's Occupational Safety and Health Administration (OSHA) that required employers to adhere to health and safety regulations for employees.

The average pay of an iron worker during the early 1800s was 75 cents a day for unskilled work and $1 a day for skilled. There were no meal breaks and workers ate on the run when their families brought them a meal.

The founder was the most important job at the furnace and the best paid, averaging about $600 a year. His job was to supervise the charging of the furnace with ore, charcoal, and limestone. Maintaining the proper temperature was of utmost importance to assure the proper melting of the ore. The founder was assisted by the keeper, who supervised operations when the founder was off duty, and by the fillers who were responsible for keeping the furnace charged. The work of the filler was backbreaking and hazardous. Working close to the furnace stack, these men were subject to severe burns and other accidents. Fillers had to endure the flame, smoke, and cinders and work in all kinds of weather, while being paid little more than common laborers.

Gutter men worked in the casting house, tapping the furnace and guiding the molten iron into roughly drawn trenches in the ground to form the long narrow iron bars called pigs. Their job included stacking the heavy "ingots" after they had cooled and hardened.

Gutter men, who in reality were often boys, also hauled away the cooling slag.

Moulders were responsible for pouring the molten iron into molds made by pressing patterns into a sand bed on the cast house floor. Moulders were considered to be highly skilled, often taking years to master their craft, and were among the best paid workmen at the furnace. The work of moulders and gutter men, however, was no less dangerous than that of the fillers, as they also endured the extreme temperatures of the furnace and the constant threat of burns from the molten iron.

Other employees, including those who worked at a distance from the village, also contributed to the success of the furnace, though they were generally paid much less than those who toiled within the ironworks. Ore diggers were responsible for extracting bog ore from the edges of streams and rivers and were generally paid by the weight of the ore they mined. Woodcutting, which was largely done in the winter, involved felling trees and hauling the timber to the coaling areas. The following ad, posted in the hope of attracting a few good woodsmen, appeared in the *Pennsylvania Evening Post* on November 14, 1776.

> *Phila.* Wood Cutters wanted at Batsto Furnace, at the Fork of Little Egg-harbor, in West New Jersey, where sober industrious men may make great wages, by cutting pine wood at two shillings and sixpence per cord, which will be given by the manager of the works, or the owner in Philadelphia.

Colliers, who turned the pinewood into charcoal, often spent months living in primitive huts in the forest tending to eight or nine charcoal kilns at a time. The average annual salary for a collier in the 1830s was $150.

Other jobs included the teamsters who carried goods to and from the landings, wheelwrights who made the wheels for wagons, farriers who shod the horses, and millers who ground corn and wheat into meal and flour. All of these workers contributed to the functioning of the village.

When the furnace went out of blast each winter, the ironworkers did whatever they could to earn their keep, including cutting ice from the pond for use in refrigeration, doing furnace and other repairs, and assisting with the woodcutting.

In 1834 there were 60–70 workers at Batsto. By 1844, there were 125, which included both the glass and iron workers. During these years there were 77 workers' homes in the village, most of them continuously occupied.

In later years when the village had turned mainly to glass production, skilled workers were lured to the village with the promise of free housing.

Glassblowing, one of the most skilled jobs at Batsto's window glass factory, was strenuous and potentially dangerous work. The combined weight of the blow pipe and glass cylinder, which the glassblowers were required to swing over a pit while infusing it with air, was 80 to 100 pounds. A fall into the swing pit was a serious matter, and one misstep could lead to the death of a worker. Batsto glassblowers in the later years are reported to have made as much as $797 a year, though they were typically responsible for paying their assistants out of this amount.

Pot makers, who made the large containers that could withstand the high temperatures of the furnace, made $35 to $50 a month. Batch makers—those who prepared the ingredients for glass—made $40 a month. Shearers, the employees charged with managing the glass furnace operation, were paid $45 a month and received a house rent free. Other less skilled glassworkers made little more than the ironworkers of a decade earlier, being paid $1 a day for their work. These workers were generally required to pay a dollar a month rent for their homes.

Cutters, the white collar workers of the glass house, were paid by the number of boxes of glass cut and packed. In 1847 Daniel Brookfield, a glass cutter at Batsto, cut 6,511 boxes of window lights at 20 cents a box. Cutters were required to pay their assistants from their own salaries.

Glass production was not done at Batsto in the summer months, and skilled workers often traveled to other locations to ply their craft during the shutdown. Some stayed at the village assisting with farming and repairs, doing whatever they could to support their families.

INDENTURED SERVANTS

An indentured servant was an individual—man or woman—who signed a contract binding him to serve a master for a specific period of time, usually two to seven years, often in return for passage from Europe. If the indentured was underage the contract was signed by a parent or guardian. In the late 18th century this was a common way for poor young people to attain free passage to America. The employer purchased the indenture from the sea captain who brought the youths over. Indentured servants earned no money once they reached their destination but were provided with food, shelter, and clothing. Though many women came to America as indentured servants, three-quarters of indentures were single men ages 18 to 27, largely unskilled. Most indentured servants worked as agricultural laborers or domestics, but some were artisans or skilled craftsmen like masons or blacksmiths, as well as miners, foundry men, forge men, carpenters, and charcoal makers.

Indentured servants were often not well treated and were sometimes worked to exhaustion. Masters had all but complete power over their indentured servants, who were virtually slaves for the period of time they were in service. Many indentures, once arrived in America, found they could not tolerate the situation and ran away. From 1704 to 1779, court records indicate that 673 indentured servants ran away from their masters in New Jersey.

In the early years, Batsto employed indentured workers and did indeed have a runaway problem, as indicated by ads like the following which ran in the *New York Gazette* and *Weekly Mercury* on July 1, 1776.

> Ten Dollars Reward.....Runaway from Batsto Furnace last Night, two Spanish Servant Men, one of them named Frances Berrara, about 30 years of age, about six Feet two Inches high, black Hair, brown Eyes, and thin Visage, takes a Quantity of snuff, his fore Teeth remarkably wide

and has a down Look: Had on, and took with him, one blue Cloth short Coat, one light brown Duffles under jacket, one Pair of new Oznabrigs Trowsers, Oznabrigs Shirt, a pair of half worn shoes, and half worn Hat with a broad Brim. The other named Francis Rodrigo....Had on and took with him....one Pair dove-colored Plush Breeches....one Pair half-worn Shoes, and an old Hat.

Whoever takes up the above runaways, and secures them in any Gaol, so that their Master, Mr. John Cox, of Burlington may have them again, or deliver them at Batsto Furnace, shall receive the above Reward and reasonable Charges.

JOSEPH BALL

N.B. This is the second Time Berrara has run away. Batsto Furnace is at the Forks of Little-Egg Harbor.

The Richards also maintained indentured servants, and an old Batsto account book shows the following disturbing entry for May 1811.

Paid for indentured black girl Maria, aged 9, to serve until she arrives at age of 21 years, $105.00. Fee for binding $1.00. Total $106.

At the time of the American Revolution indentured servants comprised approximately 10 percent of New Jersey's population of 120,000. Passage from Europe to America in the mid- to late-1700s cost £6 to £9, or $9 to $12 in today's U.S. currency.

SLAVE LABOR

While there is no evidence to show that slave labor was used in the ironworks or glassworks at Batsto, it is known that Charles Read used slave labor at his other South Jersey ironworks. In 1767 records show that Read purchased a "negro forge man named Cato" for £100. Six years later, on September 11, 1774, an ad was placed by Charles Read IV, who had recently been deeded the ironworks by his father.

TO BE SOLD BY
CHARLES READ
At AETNA, West New-Jersey
TWO FORGE NEGROES
One a good Finer, and the other a good Hammer-man

It is known, as discussed in Chapter 3, that William Richards owned at least two slaves, Andrew and Ben, who worked as house servants in the Batsto manor house. In an article published in the *Batsto Citizens Gazette* in 1980, Joseph C. Wilson, Batsto Citizen Committee member, wrote that Jesse Richards owned slaves until his death in 1854. Although New Jersey abolished slavery in 1846, the law provided that individuals could remain with their owners as apprentices, and no former slave could be divorced from such apprenticeship against his wishes.

Though it is not known if slave labor was used at the ironworks at Batsto, a store account book from 1834 through 1839 lists five workmen noted as "negroes" purchasing goods from the company store. These men could have been free laborers, slaves, or indentured servants.

The slave population in New Jersey in 1800 was 12,422 out of a total African American population of 16,824. New Jersey was the largest slave owning state in the northeast at the time. By 1830 the number of slaves in New Jersey had dropped to 2300, by 1840 to 700, and by 1860 just 18 individuals were listed as slaves.

WOMEN'S WORK AND LIVES

The pre-Revolutionary War saying, "Men may work from sun to sun but a woman's work is never done" aptly describes the life of the women who lived and worked at Batsto. While the men of Batsto worked long hours, village women worked even longer days maintaining the households and caring for the children.

Village scene in front of gristmill (photo courtesy of Budd Wilson)

Meal preparation alone took many hours of a woman's day. It required the drawing of water from a village pump, butchering small animals, cleaning and scaling fish, curing meats, cooking and tending the fireplace, growing herbs and vegetables, and making candles, soap, butter, and cheese, as well as preserving and drying fruits and vegetables for winter. The women made bread and roasted and ground coffee beans. Though the company store sold a variety of ready-made products such as dresses, meat, candles, coffee, butter, soap, etc., most of the families of Batsto could not afford such luxuries and made everything they needed from scratch.

Each worker's family was allotted a quarter acre on the south side of the lake where they could plant a garden. Generally, women and children tended the plot. Most families also kept a few chickens and maintained a pig pen behind their home.

In the time period from 1830 to 1840, food prices at the company store were as follows: pork and beef 4 cents per pound, butter 15 cents per pound, apples 4 dollars a bushel, 1 quart of molasses 12½ cents, 23 pounds of wheat flour $1, ½ pound of tea 62½ cents, two pounds of sugar 25 cents, one bushel of potatoes $1, whiskey 50 cents per gallon, and eggs 12 cents per dozen. Shoes could also be purchased, with children's shoes costing 90 cents per pair and men's heavy-duty lace-up boots valued at $5. Many residents made their own shoes, as an entire cow hide could be had for $1.50.

Laundry, which was done less often than now, required heating up large tubs of water and soaking clothing overnight. The next morning the woman of the household scrubbed the garments on rough washboards using soap made from lye, which was severely irritating to eyes and skin. Next she placed the laundry in vats of boiling water, stirring the clothes with a long pole to prevent them from developing yellow spots. Then she lifted the clothes out of the vats with a wash stick and rinsed them several times. Clothes were individually wrung out before being hung out to dry.

Cleaning was also a time-consuming and arduous chore. The soot and smoke from wood-burning stoves blackened walls and dirtied curtains and carpets. Floors had to be scrubbed, rugs beaten, and windows washed. The houses were small, however; most had only four rooms and the families owned few pieces of furniture that needed cleaning.

Most villagers owned only two or three changes of clothing; women generally stitched or knit each garment by hand.

Women oversaw all details of family life including the care and education of children. By the time children reached the age of three they were given chores to keep them from being underfoot and a burden to their mothers, who had little time to spend focused on them.

American women in the 18th and 19th centuries had virtually no individual rights and were expected to be subservient to their husbands. Women could not vote, sue or be sued, draft wills, make contracts, or buy and sell property. Upon marriage wives forfeited any property they owned to their husbands. If married women earned money outside the home it belonged to their husbands. In the rare case of divorce, fathers automatically gained custody of the children. If a husband or wife died, the remaining spouse had little time to grieve as he or she often had to remarry quickly. In those days a man needed a woman to take care of his household and children, while a woman depended upon the financial support of a man to survive.

Women could earn extra money by taking in boarders, selling eggs or baked or preserved goods to the company store, and by sewing, mending, and doing laundry for the single men of the village. Some of the women in the village also worked at the mansion doing domestic work for the ironmaster's family.

CHILDREN

Unless they were from a wealthy family, children in early rural America rarely received any formal education beyond what their families could provide. Even when a school did exist, few children attended regularly, as their labor was needed to help sustain the family. Children were not indulged and were expected to take on adult responsibilities as early as possible. Many young boys worked with their fathers in the workplace, performing menial tasks while learning the father's trade. When a child did earn a wage it was generally turned over to his parents.

Young girls were expected to help their mothers run the household. A great deal of time was spent learning to cook and sew in preparation

Village scene on Bridge Street (photo courtesy of Budd Wilson)

for one day running their own households. The older girls in the family were also expected to care for their younger siblings.

Though research for this book did not unearth any information about a school operating at Batsto prior to 1844, the minutes from an 1832 Washington Township council meeting attended by Jesse Richards indicate that $50 was appropriated for the "education of poor children." An 1830 inventory list from the schooner *Confidence* indicates that two dozen spelling books were part of the cargo being delivered to the village. It is also known that by 1810 a school operated at the nearby ironworks village of Martha, which was owned by Jesse's brother, Samuel. These few scraps of information suggest that in all probability a school operated at Batsto beginning in the early 1800s. Schools in New Jersey were not publicly funded by law prior to 1872, and parents were expected to pay tuition, generally about $1 a month for each child attending.

There is evidence that a one-room schoolhouse, recognized as Burlington County School 97, was built at Batsto Village in 1844. It is known to have been located on land on the south side of what is now Route 542. Most children only attended school for one to four years in order to learn basic literacy. Duties at home and at work in the local industries often kept children from attending school regularly.

Teachers, who taught all grades, generally first through fifth, often boarded with the parents of the children and made approximately $20 a month. In later years village children attended a school located in Pleasant Mills as well as the Crowleytown School located just beyond Crowley's Landing on the current Route 542. This building is still standing and today is used as a private residence.

By age 14, boys were often apprenticed to skilled craftsmen such as blacksmiths, weavers, or wheelwrights. Young men were bound to a master with the approval of their parents or guardians for a specified number of years, generally about seven. An apprentice lived with the master's family and assisted him and his wife in the business and in the home. In return he learned the master's trade and was provided with food, lodging, and clothing as well as basic literacy skills. Apprentices were obliged to promise the master faithful service and to not leave the premises without permission. There was no stigma attached to apprenticeship; it was accepted as a way for a young man with limited prospects to gain a marketable skill. An apprentice was often treated like a member of the family and, if he played his cards right, he might even end up marrying the master's daughter.

LEISURE TIME

Aside from fishing and hunting, which were considered work, recreation for the workers and their families was limited. In the winter, village children in their free time could be found ice skating on the frozen lake, and in the warmer months swimming in the village ponds and rivers.

Taverns, though not located in company towns, were usually built close by. Taverns were important to the people who lived in the industrial communities of the New Jersey Pine Barrens. It was where villagers went to hear all the news of the day, where they voted, and where they held special events like court hearings and weddings. During the war years, taverns became the meeting place of choice for local militias, where troops were trained and recruiters came to enlist men for military service.

Batsto baseball team (photo courtesy of Budd Wilson)

Men who labored long shifts in the Batsto ironworks and glass factory, when they had a few hours free, were apt to frequent the taverns. Overindulgence in alcohol by workers contributed to delinquency and low production, causing major problems for the owners. The liquor problem became so pervasive at Charles Read's ironworks that he used his considerable influence to pass legislation prohibiting alcohol from being sold to any employee of an ironworks within four miles of the plant.

Yet there were many taverns that operated in close proximity to Batsto. In the early years, when Read's law was in effect, workers frequented Nicholas Sooy's tavern (later renamed Washington Tavern) located on the Tuckerton Stage Road, five miles north of Batsto. Bodine's, another early Pine Barrens tavern, operated where the Tuckerton stage road crossed the Wading River. Bodine's was a frequent haunt of the Martha furnace workers. In later years, there was also Jonathan Cramer's tavern at the Mount, a few miles north of the works, and the Thompson Tavern located at Quakerbridge on the road to the Atsion Ironworks. Abe Nichol's tavern, located less than a mile east of the village, operated near his shipping landing on the Mullica River.

Taverns were important not only to the local men and women, but to anyone traveling long distances on horseback or by stagecoach. Most taverns were built on stage lines where weary travelers could stop to refresh their horses and themselves, with room and board available to those on overnight journeys.

Though taverns were a favored place to enjoy a few hours of leisure, an even greater number of Batsto residents spent their scant free time attending services at the Batsto Pleasant Mills church. The church was built in 1808 on the site of a former log church built by Elijah Clark in 1762. Joseph Ball, who at the time owned the property where the church stands, turned the deed over to seven trustees, including William and Jesse Richards, "for the use of ministers and preachers of any Christian denomination." However, the church appears to have been used only by those of the Protestant faiths.

Jesse Richards, his wife Sarah, and many of his children are buried in the cemetery next to the church. Revolutionary and Civil War patriots are buried there as well. Though the church didn't have its own pastor, itinerant preachers traveling a rural circuit would often officiate there. When such preachers came to sermonize at the little chapel they often stayed with the Richards family. Sometimes church attendance was so robust that Jesse Richards would send his six-mule-team open wagon to be used as a pulpit. The wagon pulpit would be placed between the two front church doors so that everyone, both inside and outside, could hear the sermon.

In the early years, Catholic families who were living at Batsto conducted services in their homes. In 1826 Jesse Richards donated land in Pleasant Mills to the Catholic families of the village and made a contribution toward the construction of a church. Work was quickly begun and construction of St. Mary's of the Assumption was completed the following year, making it the first Catholic Church in New Jersey to be built south of Trenton. Once again the Richards family opened its home to traveling priests who officiated at the church when they were in the area.

St Mary's was destroyed by a forest fire in April 1900 and today just a few tombstones remain to mark the site.

Batsto Pleasant Mills Church (photo by Albert D. Horner)

St. Mary's of the Assumption (photo courtesy of the New Jersey State Archives)

St. Mary's cemetery, present day (photo by Albert D. Horner)

The Wharton Years

Without Joseph Wharton, the Pinelands as we know it today would not exist. Wharton began buying land along the lower reaches of the Mullica and Batsto Rivers in 1873 in pursuit of a plan to raise sugar beets. In 1876 he acquired the Batsto estate at a fire sale and would continue to purchase land in the New Jersey Pine Barrens until shortly before his death in 1909. Soon after acquiring Batsto, Wharton hired Elias Wright to manage his estate as well as to act as his agent in acquiring and surveying further land purchases in the area. Wright spent 30 years surveying and buying some 300 separate parcels of land for Wharton. Often, entire towns—frequently deserted—such as Martha, Harrisville, Atsion, and Hampton, were included in these transactions, which would ultimately comprise real estate holdings in three counties and nine townships.

Though it is commonly believed that Joseph Wharton bought his New Jersey Pine Barrens properties in order to acquire water rights, which he could then sell to the cities of Philadelphia and Camden, it appears that this idea did not occur to him until the early 1890s. Wharton clearly sought to make a financial profit from his Pinelands holdings, whether it was through the raising of crops and cattle, lumbering, or the sale of water. None of these ventures, however, ever led to much financial gain. And although he hoped to make money from his land acquisitions, it was his accumulation of this sprawling wasteland that created his greatest legacy: the conservation of a vast and unique wilderness area known as the Wharton Tract. Situated within the heart of the Pine Barrens, today's Wharton State Forest encompasses approximately 127,000 acres, making it the largest state forest in New Jersey.

THE EDUCATION OF JOSEPH WHARTON

Joseph Wharton was born in 1826, the fifth child of Deborah and William Wharton, ministers in the Society of Friends. Wharton's parents had no gainful employment and lived off fortunes inherited from their families who had been wealthy Philadelphia merchants. Though Quakers held as one of their core beliefs the act of living simply, they were not bound to poverty but rather believed wealth should not be used frivolously but to help others.

Deborah and William met as children while attending the same Quaker meeting. Deborah's father, Samuel Fisher, gave the couple a house at 130 Spruce Street in Philadelphia as a wedding present, and this is where the family would live for many years. Over an eighteen-year period, Deborah gave birth to five girls and five boys.

Joseph, when he was not attending a Quaker boarding school, received private tutoring at the Spruce Street home. In 1834 his grandfather, Charles Wharton, gave William and Deborah his Schuylkill River country estate known as Bellevue. Located several miles northwest of Philadelphia, Bellevue was where the family spent its summers.

The Wharton family was involved with the Hicksite Quaker faction that seceded from the traditional Society of Friends, which they referred to as Orthodox. Among their values, the more liberal Hicksites advocated a rural lifestyle. In keeping with their practice, at age 16 Joseph was sent to live on a farm located in Chester County, Pennsylvania, owned by Joseph and Abigail Walton, Quaker family friends of the Whartons. The young man spent three years with the Waltons learning about farming techniques. As part of this arrangement his father paid his board while he was there.

The Walton family worked 16-hour days during the planting and harvesting seasons. It was a hard life but Joseph took to it, writing home of his fascination with the changing tasks as the seasons progressed. By the time he left the farm three years later he stood 6 feet tall and weighed 145 pounds. He maintained a healthy lifestyle by exercising regularly, keeping routine sleeping and working hours, and maintaining a healthy diet. At some point during his last year on the farm he became a strict vegetarian, giving up meat, milk, and salt. Alarmed at what they viewed as a radical decision, the family lectured him endlessly about his diet, Deborah Wharton eventually writing that she would "think thee in need of guardianship" if he continued on this path. Joseph ended his dietary experiments soon after, suggesting that he took his mother's words seriously.

During the winters when the farm tasks slowed, Joseph Wharton returned to live with his family. During these months he studied

Joseph Wharton as a young man (photographer unknown)

chemistry in the Philadelphia laboratory of Martin Hans Boye, one of the area's leading scientists. After leaving the farm for good, he became an apprentice at the Quaker mercantile and importing firm of Waln and Leeming. Over the next two years, while receiving an allowance from his father, Joseph learned accounting and became proficient in bookkeeping and business management.

The Wharton family had large land holdings throughout New York, Pennsylvania, and Indiana, which had been inherited from Joseph's paternal and maternal grandparents. These holdings were rich in natural resources, such as timber, coal, iron, and salt, as well as a good supply of water power. During his lifetime, William Wharton managed these resources and after his death Joseph would take on the responsibility. Throughout the years, William was very generous toward his sons as well as his sons-in-law, helping them to get started in various businesses. This was the Quaker way.

WHARTON'S DESTINY UNFOLDS

In 1847, when Joseph was 21, he joined his older brother Rodman in a venture to refine and market cottonseed oil. The business failed and the brothers dissolved their partnership in 1849. Soon after, Joseph found an opportunity in brick manufacturing. By the spring of 1849 he had entered into a partnership with the owner of several large brickyards to sell bricks and brick-making machines. Although he learned a great deal from his involvement with this enterprise, by 1853 he had begun to doubt its prospects for making money and sold his share of the company.

In 1849 Joseph became engaged to Anna Lovering, the younger sister of his brother Charles's wife, Mary. Anna, whose family were also members of the Society of Friends, was slim, pretty, reserved, and intelligent. Her father, Joseph Lovering, was a wealthy industrialist who had developed an innovative method of refining sugar and was among the leading manufacturers in the field. Lovering's interest and experience in sugar making would later be instrumental in Wharton's purchase of his Pine Barrens land. The Loverings owned a large mansion called Oak Hill, which was located near Germantown, Pennsylvania.

Joseph and Anna's engagement lasted four years and, on June 15, 1854, they were married at Oak Hill in the presence of 60 witnesses, all members of the two families. By this time Joseph was managing a mining operation for the Pennsylvania and Lehigh Zinc Company near Bethlehem, Pennsylvania. Later he would manage the company's zinc oxide works. This job required him initially to have many long separations from Anna, who remained living with her parents in Oak Hill even though the couple had purchased a home at 33 South 12th Street in Philadelphia.

By 1863 when Wharton left the Pennsylvania and Lehigh Zinc Company, he and Anna had started a family, their first daughter, Joanna, having been born in 1859. Two more daughters would follow: Mary in 1862 and Anna in 1868. After leaving the company, Wharton formed the American Nickel Works, hoping to profit from the use of nickel in coins. Based in Camden, New Jersey, the American Nickel Works would eventually produce the only nickel used in the United States as well as a significant percentage of the world's supply.

While Wharton was operating his nickel works he sat on the board of directors of Bethlehem Iron, and it was under his direction that the company was renamed the Bethlehem Steel Company. In the late 1870s he used money made in his nickel works to increase his holdings in Bethlehem Steel, and by 1899 he had become the company's largest stockholder.

SUGAR BEETS

In the mid-19th century most of the sugar consumed in the United States was sourced from Cuban sugar cane. Like many other American entrepreneurs, Joseph Wharton was interested in developing a new industry to produce sugar in the United States. His interest in sugar was likely kindled by his father-in-law, Joseph Lovering, who had a long and successful involvement in the industry. Elsewhere in the world, agriculturists had been successfully experimenting with the cultivation of sugar beets, from which they were able to extract sugar. In 1873 Wharton traveled to Europe, recording in detail his visits to an experimental sugar beet farm in England.

L–R: Joseph Wharton's wife Anna, daughters Anna and Joanna, Joseph, and daughter Mary (photo courtesy of the New Jersey State Archives)

With this enterprise in mind, Wharton began to acquire land in the Pinelands of southern New Jersey, accumulating about 50,000 acres by the end of 1873. Occasional remarks in his correspondence indicate that he was fascinated by the Pine Barrens, where as a young man he and his brothers had made frequent excursions on horseback. When Wharton began making these purchases it was the end of an industrial boom in the Pine Barrens, and land was cheap. Soon he needed someone to take charge of his burgeoning Pine Barrens land holdings, and when he met retired Union Civil War general Elias Wright, he knew he'd found his man.

Elias Wright was born in Durham, New York, the son of a farmer. He attributed most of his education to self-study and life experience gained on his father's farm. He initially had ambitions to be a schoolteacher, but after settling in Atlantic City, New Jersey, in 1852, he pursued a career in civil engineering and surveying.

With the outbreak of the Civil War, Wright was commissioned a captain after raising and equipping a company called the Home Guards. Although not regular army, his men fought in the Battle of Bull Run. The Home Guards were later mustered into the 4th New Jersey Infantry.

By 1862 Wright was promoted to First Lieutenant and during his time in the Union Army he saw a great deal of battle. At one point during the war he was captured by the Confederates and imprisoned at Libby Prison in Richmond, Virginia, but he was freed after seven weeks as part of a prisoner exchange.

Following his release, Wright continued to serve with distinction. He was severely injured during one skirmish, but he recovered and went on to fight in such important battles as Antietam, Fredericksburg, Salem Heights, and Chaffin's Farm. In 1865 he was given the rank of Brevet Brigadier General and decorated for gallant and meritorious service.

When the war ended, Elias Wright resigned his command and returned to the New Jersey Pine Barrens, which he now called home. In 1873 he began his lengthy and productive association with Joseph Wharton, working as his agent in acquiring land, researching property titles, and surveying his growing land holdings in the Pine Barrens.

Joseph Wharton planted his first large crop of beets in 1877, one year after purchasing 36,000 acres of the Batsto estate. That year he renovated the gristmill at Batsto with the purpose of extracting the juice and boiling it down to crude sugar. The following account of this process appeared in the *Hammonton Item* on November 17, 1877.

> The beets are pulled and stacked in the field without trimming; they are then hauled to the factory and weighed; the tops are then cut off, the beets washed, weighed and then put in the grinding machine, which grinds them into a fine pulp, the machine grinding them as fast as a man can shovel them in. The pulp is then taken up, weighed again and put into a large cylinder (making 2,500 revolutions

Aerial view of Batsto (photo courtesy of the New Jersey State Archives)

per minute) which extracts all the juice; the pulp is then taken out, weighed again, salted and packed away to feed the cattle during the winter. The juice is pumped into tanks through filters, then into large iron kettles, where it is boiled; then through the boiling kettles again, the chemist testing it in its various stages. When it is boiled down to the consistency of good molasses, it is drawn off to barrels and hogsheads and sent to the city for refining. The establishment gives employment to about twenty-five hands, and runs day and night.

In January 1878 Wharton advertised for sugar beets from other farmers, providing extensive directions on how the crop should be cultivated. For unknown reasons the sugar beet experiment did not continue; there is no mention of it in Wharton's account books beyond March 1878. It has been speculated that Wharton may have stopped his sugar beet experiment too soon as he made one crucial mistake: Grinding the beats as he did, rather than slicing them, produces a cloudy syrup which adds to filtering problems. Another possibility, as suggested by Wharton's daughter Joanna Lippincott in *Biographical Memoranda Concerning Joseph Wharton 1826–1909*, is that the sugar beet experiment failed because the New Jersey Pine Barrens soil and climate proved unsuitable for this particular crop.

Wharton did, however, restore the manor home at Batsto under the direction of Elias Wright and at a cost of $40,000. Wright employed the architectural firm of Sloan and Balderston of Philadelphia, who remodeled the mansion in the Italianate architectural style, which was popular at the time.

The restoration was finished by May 1880, in time for the manse to serve as a convalescent home for Wharton's daughter, Mary, who is reported by Wharton biographer W. Ross Yates to have suffered a nervous breakdown. Wharton felt that the clean air and quiet, restful surroundings were just what his daughter needed to recover.

Joseph Wharton and family at the mansion (photo courtesy of Budd Wilson)

Mary came to Batsto in the late spring of 1881 when she was 19 years old, accompanied by a caretaker named Mrs. McClure, and would spend a year at Batsto convalescing. In a letter dated May 25, 1881, Anna Wharton wrote to Mary expressing the following encouraging sentiments.

> "I am glad to think of thee now, in such an attractive spot with so kind a caretaker and I trust thee is already reaping the benefits of the lovely and invigorating air of Batsto. I congratulate thee on again taking dinner at the dining room table, and hope thee will be supplied with plenty of good food."

Though the sugar beet experiment had ended, Wharton's acquisition of pinelands property continued, as did other minor farming on his Pine Barrens land. In 1881 Wharton took up cattle breeding. He purchased a herd of beef cattle that he initially grazed at Batsto and later on his land near Washington, New Jersey, just five miles north of Batsto. As of January 11, 1884, Wharton's livestock included 113 cattle at Batsto and 50 at Washington. Eventually he would maintain 400 cattle at Washington. The cattle grazed there, reportedly running free as far as Quaker Bridge. Unfortunately, this experiment also did not go well, as Pine Barrens foliage, while nourishing for deer, does not provide good forage for cattle.

WHARTON'S WATER PLAN

Sometime in the early 1890s Wharton devised a plan to sell the pristine waters in the streams and rivers on his Pine Barrens land to the cities of Camden and Philadelphia. He knew both cities needed access to pure water, particularly Philadelphia, which during the 1890s had the highest death rate from typhoid fever and other water-borne diseases of any city in America. Raw sewage was being dumped into the Delaware and Schuylkill rivers near where Philadelphia was obtaining its drinking water. At the time Wharton was devising his water plan, Philadelphia was considering two solutions: obtaining new sources of supply and/or using filtration beds, though the latter method was not yet completely proven.

It was estimated that the daily flow of water on Wharton's Pine Barrens land was almost 900 million gallons—six times the amount used by Philadelphia and Camden combined. As his plan unfolded, Wharton began buying more land in the Pine Barrens, his largest purchase being the Atsion tract (23,000 acres), which was owned by the Raleigh family at the time. By 1892 he owned approximately 150 square miles of land in the New Jersey Pine Barrens. At around the same time, the city of Philadelphia condemned and seized the Wharton family mansion at Bellevue for the purpose of building a reservoir that would hold potable water. Although this reservoir never materialized, perhaps the seizure of his family home increased Wharton's motivation to develop an alternative water supply for the city.

Working with an engineer, Wharton drafted a plan to bring water to the cities. In March 1892 he printed a pamphlet entitled "The Best Water for Philadelphia" detailing his plan for creating the South Jersey Water Company. The plan called for damming up all the rivers and streams on his Pine Barrens properties to create large reservoirs, then pumping the water to Camden and Philadelphia.

Philadelphia and Camden showed little interest in Wharton's plan, indicating they did not want water that someone else held title to. Shortly thereafter, Philadelphia installed a city-wide water filtration system, and New Jersey passed a law that prevented the export of water from the state, putting an end to Wharton's scheme.

On February 26, 1894, a discouraged Joseph Wharton wrote Elias Wright to say, in part, "I ... have very little appetite for Jersey land and have in fact much more of it than money." He continued, "I spent yesterday about the Jersey property and have seldom felt so discouraged about it ... I intend to buy no more land, and to cut down on expenses." He concluded his letter by saying, "The water scheme has no sign of life in it—no more than anything in Jersey."

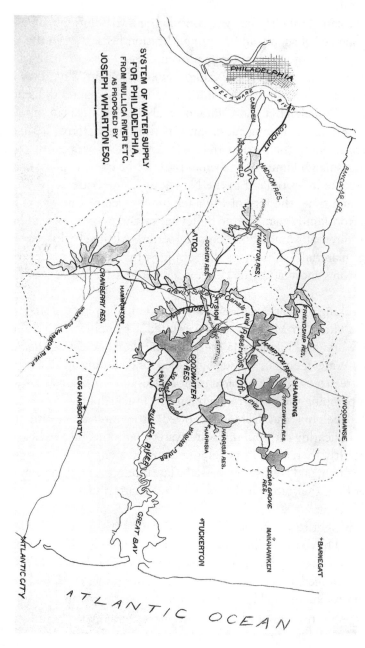

Wharton's water plan (courtesy of the Batsto Museum)

Joseph Wharton in his later years (photographer unknown)

WHARTON'S LATER ENTERPRISES

Even with the water plan seemingly dead and in spite of what he had told Elias Wright, Wharton continued to purchase land in the Pine Barrens. In 1902 he engaged Fredric Meier, a professional forester, to help him manage his growing New Jersey wilderness holdings. Meier not only convinced Wharton that forestry could be profitable, but was instrumental in the development of a 1000-acre tract demonstrating how a forest could be effectively managed. By 1903 Meier had established a nursery at Atsion and planted 10,000 seedlings each of pine, European larch, Norway and Douglas spruce, western Catalpa, black locust, and black walnut. Although the project showed promise early on, in spite of Meier's expertise it did not ultimately prove profitable and was abandoned.

In 1901 Andrew Etheridge, Wharton's farm manager at Atsion, under Wharton's direction, began experimenting with peanut cultivation.

Initial results were promising, and in 1906 it was reported that Wharton's land had produced one hundred bushels of peanuts. In later years, lumbering and cranberry production were the two enterprises Wharton and his heirs depended upon to pay the estate's bills. The sawmill at Batsto was rebuilt in 1882, and products produced there included shingle butts, rails, telegraph poles, boat planks, siding for housing, and fencing.

During these years the Wharton family continued to use the Batsto mansion as an occasional weekend retreat. Full time caretakers, who resided in the east wing of the mansion, were always on hand to look after the family when they came for a visit.

In 1881, Wharton built a mansion the family called Ontalauna on land he had previously purchased, several miles north of Philadelphia near his in-laws' Oak Hill estate. The Whartons made Ontalauna their main residence, selling the Spruce Street home. That same year Wharton built a summer residence in Rhode Island in the middle of Narragansett Bay on Conanicut Island. The family called this 30-acre retreat Marbella (it would later be known as Horsehead) and moved in the summer of 1884.

Every summer thereafter, from July to the end of September, was spent swimming, fishing, and sailing at the private resort which they shared with many visitors including a number of Wharton's business associates. When Wharton's father-in-law died shortly after the family moved into Ontalauna, Wharton purchased Oak Hill from the estate and gave it to his daughter Joanna as a wedding present.

On August 27, 1896, Wharton offered his entire Pine Barrens estate for sale to New York City businessman Peter Garrahan for $1.2 million. At the time, Wharton listed his property as consisting of more than 100,000 acres. In 1897 Garrahan was still trying to buy the property, but for some unknown reason a deal was never consummated.

During the years Wharton owned Batsto, descendants of those who had worked in the iron furnaces and glass plants continued to live in the village, some working in the sawmill or doing odd jobs around the estate. In the beginning Wharton charged villagers $2 a month rent for their homes. By the turn of the century rent was $5 a month and after WWII it jumped to $15 a month. In the early

Ontalauna (photo courtesy of Bill Schaal)

Marbella (photo courtesy of Bill Schaal)

years, 1882–1893, Elias Wright's brother George was Batsto's farm manager before being replaced by Alonzo Norton. The farm manager was responsible for the village store as well as farm operations, and indirectly supervised lumbering operations. By 1910 the village store had closed, but a villager named Isaac Peterson opened a small store in the "Spy House" where he sold articles the villagers did not produce at home including molasses, coffee, kerosene, sugar, flour, and yard goods.

In 1881, Joseph Wharton, who had not himself attended college, endowed the University of Pennsylvania with $500,000 to establish a "School of Finance and Economy." That esteemed school is known today as the Wharton School of Business. It was not the first time the Whartons had invested in higher education, as in 1869 Joseph Wharton, his mother, and a group of like-minded Quakers had founded Swarthmore College. In later years, this man of many talents would write and have published several books on finance and business, as well as a book featuring his own poetry and speeches.

Wharton's business interests were certainly not confined to southern New Jersey. During the years he was purchasing land in the Pine Barrens he also bought three iron furnaces in northern New Jersey. He purchased the Andover Iron Company in Phillipsburg in 1868, the Warren Furnace in Hackettstown in 1879, and the Port Oram Furnace in 1882.

From 1885 through the 1890s, Wharton owned a menhaden (popularly known as mossbunker) fish oil processing plant on Crab Island in the Great Bay off Tuckerton, New Jersey. Menhaden oil was valued for such purposes as softening leather. After the menhaden were squeezed for oil, the remaining fish scraps were prepared and sold as fertilizer. During these years Wharton also owned gold and silver mines in Arizona and Nevada.

Wharton died at his Ontalauna estate on January 11, 1909, several years after suffering a stroke. He was cremated and his ashes were placed in the Laurel Hill cemetery in Philadelphia. At the time of his death his estate was valued at over nine million dollars. After his death the Pine Barrens estate was managed by the Girard Trust Company.

Wharton's heirs continued to enjoy short visits to the estate. During an interview when he was in his nineties, Nicholas Biddle Jr., a great-grandson of Joseph Wharton, talked of visiting Batsto with his wife and 10 friends in the 1940s. Biddle smiled when he shared how everyone was intrigued with the place and how he and his guests enjoyed a day canoeing and picnicking on the Batsto River. After they returned from their day's outing, Biddle and the others organized a baseball game on the mansion lawn and later, after dinner, cleared off the dining room table and used it to play ping pong. Biddle added that the mansion caretakers, John and Julia Herman, prepared excellent meals and generally made everyone quite comfortable.

In 1912 public officials in the New Jersey government proposed that the state purchase the Wharton lands for $1 million. A referendum was presented in 1915, but the proposition was defeated by the voters. In 1917 12,000 acres of the Wharton lands were sold to the Atlantic Loading Company—referred to as Amatol—for a WWI shell loading plant.

In the early 1950s the U.S. Air Force considered purchasing the Wharton estate for a jet airport supply depot. The governor at the time, Alfred E. Driscoll, fought the plan. The legislature joined in the fight and voted to set aside $2 million to purchase 56,000 acres of the estate. The following year another 40,000 acres were purchased for $1 million. This time the voters of New Jersey supported the purchase.

In the final years of his life, with the assistance of Fredric Meier, Joseph Wharton began a rational forestry program and, as if by accident, became a conservationist. Although he had worked long and hard to exploit the natural resources on his Pine Barrens properties, in the end he emerged as a good steward of the land who helped to preserve it for generations to come.

The Village

The quiet, picturesque village of Batsto, located on the southern edge of the Wharton State Forest, has a pastoral atmosphere, more reminiscent of its time spent as an agrarian country estate than of the bustling industrial center of long ago. On a hill in this remote hamlet stands a majestic Victorian mansion surrounded by ancient sycamore trees. Near the mansion are barns and other stone and clapboard structures that long ago were teeming with life. Built far from the mainstream to be near the natural resources needed by the early companies that operated here, this isolated community was forced to be self-sufficient. Workers were brought in and housing was built for them and their families. A village sawmill produced lumber to build the structures and other wooden items needed by the town and its industries. A company farm produced much of the food that was needed. The village gristmill ground the wheat and corn grown by the farmers into flour and meal.

There was a piggery for rendering hogs and large barns to house the village horses, mules, and cows. Wheelwright and blacksmith shops made the wheels and rims for wagons and other horse-drawn vehicles. The company store, located in the heart of the village, was where the workers and their families went to purchase the groceries, clothing, and other items they were unable to produce at home.

If these now-silent buildings could speak they would tell of a time when Batsto was home to hundreds of people, a time when the village vibrated with life. Batsto Village, with its restored mansion, workers' homes, company store, sawmill, gristmill, and other village structures is an open-air history museum for everyone interested in learning more about life in 19th-century America.

MANSION CONSTRUCTION

Legend has it that a grand mansion called Whitcomb Manor existed at Batsto as early as the mid-1700s. Some believe that this manor home stood on the very hill where the current mansion now sits. It is said to have belonged to Israel Pemberton, a Philadelphia business-man and an uncle of Charles Read, Batsto's first ironmaster. Perhaps this connection to the vast wilderness is what first drew Read to the area. Perhaps it explains how he learned of the abundant natural resources that existed here.

Today's Batsto mansion, with its distinctive Victorian appearance, is a composite of several different periods of construction. Though there is no conclusive documentation confirming the construction dates of the various sections, the prevailing archaeological view is that there were three episodes of building and modification.

Jack Cresson, an archaeologist who completed work on the mansion in the 1980s, believes that the oldest surviving section of the foundation may have been constructed during the period when Batsto was owned by John Cox or Joseph Ball (1770 to 1779). A newspaper clipping from the *Pennsylvania Packet* of April 15, 1784, advertising the sale of Batsto, supports this claim, referring to "a large commodious mansion house on a hill overlooking the pond."

Cresson believes the mansion foundation remained unaltered until the early 19th century, when the second building episode occurred on the southeastern end. Cresson concluded that this construction occurred around 1812, during the period when Jesse Richards was managing the ironworks.

The third building episode was carried out by Joseph Wharton during the last quarter of the 19th century. Wharton's renovation was completed in the Italianate style of architecture, which was popular at the time.

Work done in the 1960s by architectural historian G. Edwin Brumbaugh concluded that the central part of the mansion where the warming kitchen is now located was the original section of the house, and that the eastern section—the caretaker's wing—was built in 1815. Brumbaugh believed that the western section, which includes both the north and south parlors, was added in 1830 by

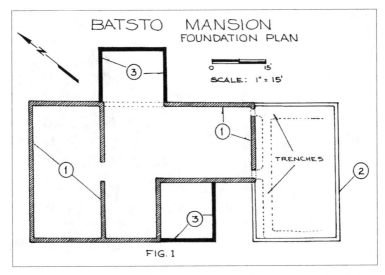

BATSTO MANSION
FOUNDATION PLAN

SCALE: 1" = 15'

TRENCHES

FIG. 1

Three episodes of mansion construction (drawing courtesy of Jack Cresson)

Jesse Richards. Brumbaugh and Cresson agree on the timing of the Wharton era restoration.

When Wharton purchased Batsto in 1876 the mansion was in a dilapidated state. Under Elias Wright's supervision, the Philadelphia architectural firm of Sloan and Balderston was hired to draw up plans to restore the mansion. Wharton's restoration, which cost $40,000, completely rebuilt the interior of the home. The entryway was enlarged to include a grand staircase. A section of the northern end was extended to add a large dining room with a master bedroom suite directly above. The restoration added three bathrooms, two in the family wing and one in the caretaker section. It also added indoor plumbing and central heating as well as interior gas lines. An 84-foot tower, which included two bedrooms and a small library, was built to house a 1200-gallon wooden water tank as well as a forest fire lookout. A hydraulic ram pumped water from a well located near the gristmill to the mansion's tower. The fire look-out, originally an open space, was enclosed in glass in 1919.

Wharton divided the house into two separate dwellings. During his ownership the eastern section became the caretaker's living

Batsto mansion (photo by Albert D. Horner)

quarters. He added gables and casement windows and a wrap-around porch on the south and west sides. A new front entrance was created on the building's south side. Wharton also added a fourth story to the eastern caretaker's end. The mansion today has 36 rooms, 12 of which are located in the caretaker's section.

Wharton's restoration included a tunnel that connected to a window well under the dining room. The tunnel is brick lined and has an arched ceiling approximately 4' high and 4' wide. It continues under the cellar floor for 25' where it divides into two smaller tunnels. Though the purpose for this tunnel is not known, there is speculation that it was built to promote ventilation and provide a constant supply of fresh air into the mansion. During the late 1900s it was believed that disease was caused by breathing air that someone had already breathed. Wharton's tunnel may have been built with this presumption in mind.

Another low-ceilinged room above the third floor landing in the tower hallway has long caused speculation for those interested in the Batsto mansion. Some say it was a "safe room" where escaping slaves were harbored in the years prior to Emancipation. However, since we know the Richards owned slaves, it seems unlikely that Batsto was a way station on the Underground Railroad. Most experts believe the room is a by-product of Wharton's remodeling and didn't exist before 1878.

MANSION INTERIOR

When first entering the mansion, visitors are ushered into a grand hallway, which includes the staircase added to the house during the Wharton restoration of 1878. The steps of the staircase are made of ash wood, the wainscoting is walnut, and the rest of the construction is done in oak and butternut.

To the left of the entry hallway is the south parlor, once used for teas, formal gatherings, and after-dinner parties. It is separated from the connecting north parlor, which was used for less formal occasions, by pocket doors. Most of the furnishings in the two parlors are not original to the mansion but are antiques dating from the mid- to late 19th century. The secretary and desk in the north parlor, however, did belong to Joseph Wharton.

Dining room (photo by Albert D. Horner)

The dining room contains a number of Wharton family pieces including the dining table, the sideboard, and two leather-upholstered chairs at the back of the room. The sideboard was fashioned from oak taken from Wharton's eldest daughter Joanna Lippincott's Oak Hill estate, a property given to her by her parents as a wedding present.

Next to the dining room is the warming kitchen. During the Wharton era the main kitchen would have been located in the caretaker's side of the mansion. In the Richards era, cooking was done in the basement. The warming kitchen was only used for final preparation and warming of the food before it was served in the dining room. In the back of the warming kitchen is a row of bells, which were originally located in the caretaker's section. The bells were connected to brass pulls in all of the rooms used by the family. When the bell handle was moved left to right, a wire in the wall would go taut causing a bell to ring in the caretaker's section. The tone of the bell and its position told the caretaker which room wanted service.

Underneath the stairway, on the first floor of Wharton's tower addition is a library. It is believed that Elias Wright may have used this room as an office. The sink was probably installed for his use, as at the time arsenic was placed on the top of books to control boll weevils, known to eat the paper, which was made from cotton and linen.

In the library is a stuffed green parrot that originally belonged to the Wharton family. The family gave the parrot, who was named Polly, to the Bozarth family—Batsto caretakers in the 1930s and '40s—after Wharton's daughter Joanna died. A news article in the *Atlantic City Press* noted that Polly was still going strong at 80 and in fact had just laid her first egg. By then she was living with Julia and John Herman, Batsto caretakers from 1945 until a few years after the state took possession of the property. Polly, who talked, sang, and danced, was celebrated for her salty vocabulary.

Halfway between the second and third floors, a hallway to the right leads to what may have been a family room during the Richards era. This room lacks central heating vents or a servant bell pull—amenities that were widely installed during the Wharton restoration—and is thus believed to have been used as servants' quarters during this period. (Servants had only a fireplace or small portable stove for heat.) As the room is close to the family bedchambers, it may have accommodated a servant of some importance.

Continuing up the stairs and turning to the right, one finds the bedchamber of Joseph and Anna Wharton. This bedroom, located directly above the dining room, features a sitting area located near a coal-fired fireplace. During the late 19th century the bedchambers of the wealthy were considered more than a place to sleep and were often used for eating meals, reading, and writing letters. The bed in the room is 6' square with a high headboard. In Wharton's time it was commonly thought that respiratory diseases such as tuberculosis and pneumonia, which were prevalent, could be prevented by sleeping in an upright position. The large headboard allowed for pillows to be piled high so that a person could easily sleep in a sitting position.

There are servant bell pulls on either side of the bed, along with a speaking tube that served as an early intercom system. To the right of the bed is a doorway leading to a bathroom, which is brightened by a light shaft that connects to a glass panel on the roof.

Walking back to the stairway you will see two connecting bedchambers on the west side. These bedrooms date back to the Richards era. The bed and desk in the south chamber belonged to the Richards family at one time, though it is not known if they were ever used in the mansion.

The hall bathroom, installed by Wharton, was used by family members and their guests. A copper-covered zinc tub and a toilet tank placed high on the wall were fixtures common to that era.

Next to the bathroom is the second floor tower bedchamber. This room was used by family members or their guests, as evidenced by the central heating system and servant bell pull. Exposed piping in the right corner walls of this room is part of an indoor fire extinguishing system that was fed by the water tank in the tower.

Between the second and third floor is a hallway leading to the right. Off this hallway is a two-room servant's suite. The two rooms are set up as a sitting room and a bedroom with a fireplace.

As you make your way up the stairway to the third floor, a door directly on your right at the top of the stairs opens to a room that is currently used for storage and is not open to the public. This room, directly above the Wharton master bedroom, has central heating and a servant bell and was no doubt used by the family or its guests.

The large room located at the top of the stairway dates to the Richards era and was probably used as servants' quarters at that time. Joseph Wharton added the large windows at the front and sides of the room, giving it added light and an increased sense of space. During the Wharton era the room was used for family leisure activities such as board games.

A doorway from this floor provides access to the tower. A bedroom equipped with a servant call system and central heating is located directly behind the tower door. Above this bedroom is the 1200-gallon water tank and, above that, a spiral staircase leads to the fire lookout tower.

The mansion appears today as it would have when the Wharton family owned Batsto. Mansion tours provided by knowledgeable guides, known as docents, do not currently visit the tower or the caretaker's section of the house, which serve as office space for state employees with New Jersey DEP's Division of Parks and Forestry. In fact, only 15 of the mansion's 36 rooms are open to the public on guided tours as of this writing.

THE MILLS

The gristmill that stands today was built in 1828 by Jesse Richards, though we know there was a gristmill on the property at least as early as 1783. For any 19th-century village in this area, a gristmill was a necessity; it was the place where farmers brought their corn and wheat to be ground into meal and flour. The Batsto gristmill also milled small grains like rye, buckwheat, and barley though wheat and corn were its mainstays. The gristmill was originally operated by a wooden water wheel that turned when water was released from the pond into a millrace. When the wheel turned it powered gearing that ran the mill machinery. Archaeological work done in 1957 concluded that

Batsto Mansion

Visitor Center

Entranceway

Front Parlor

View from Back Parlor

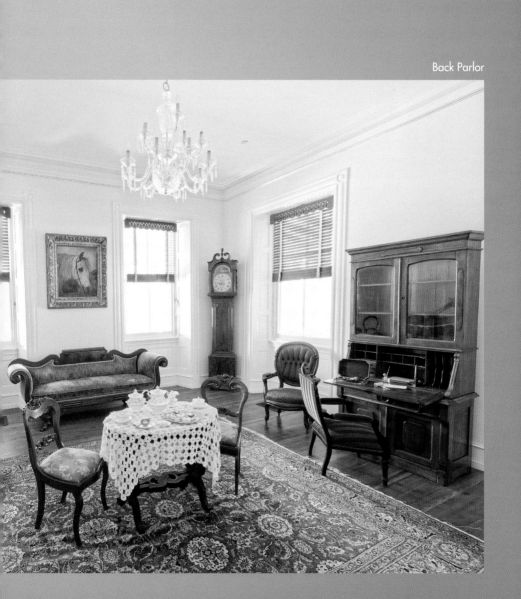

Back Parlor

Warming Kitchen

Dining Room

Polly the Parrot

Library

Joseph and Anna Wharton's Bed Chamber

Wharton Era Bathroom

Richards Era Bedrooms

Second Floor Tower Bedroom

Water Tank

Tower Steps to Forest Fire Look-out

Servant's Suite

Leisure Room Wharton Era

Company Store

Company Store Interior

View From Mansion Tower

Post Office

Post Office Interior

Blacksmith and Wheel-Wright Shops

Mule Barn

Piggery

Ice House

Nature Center

Alonzo Norton House

Trail

Batsto Lake

Ore Boat

Stagecoach

Carriage Barn

Carpenter's Tool Display

Sawmill Interior

Sawmill

Workers' House, First Floor

Second Floor

Workers' Double House

The gristmill (photo by Albert D. Horner)

the water wheel was replaced by a water-driven turbine at an early date in the 19th century. The turbine was connected to a series of wooden gears and pulleys in the mill, which controlled the huge grinding stones.

The corn crib, where corn was stored and shelled, was built during the Wharton era. The crib was rat-proofed by means of heavy mesh screen and by being set on cast-iron water pipes inches above the ground. A platform stretched above both sides of the crib. Huskers stood on the upper level, operating a sheller that removed the kernels from the cobs. After the shelling, the kernels were sent down a chute that connected with the third floor of the gristmill. Threshing—the process of extracting wheat germ from the husks—was done in the threshing barn, which stood next to the horse stable.

The milling process involved feeding grain into a hopper that stood directly above the two milling stones. As the grain fell through an opening to a gap between the stones, the top or "running stone" revolved over the lower stationary stone. The speed of the revolving stone was regulated by controlling the amount of water fed to the turbine. The distance between the stones was adjusted by the miller to accommodate different grain sizes. If the milling stones were set too close together the stone and grain could become overheated and would emit an odor. The miller had to pay close attention to this process, a job from which arose the age-old admonition to "keep your nose to the grindstone."

Furrows cut into the face of each millstone allowed the meal or flour to flow to the edges of the stones. A brush on the edge of the runner stone then swept the product into a chute that directed it into bins on the floor below. After further processing the flour and meal were placed in burlap bags, then taken to the store to be sold.

In the 1830s, the Batsto gristmill was one of 400 such mills known to be operating in New Jersey. In 1850 alone the mill produced 250 tons of flour and feed. Rebuilt by the state in the 1960s, Batsto's gristmill is still able to process corn and wheat today.

The Batsto sawmill produced the lumber used to build the structures, furniture, and other wooden items needed by the village. Cedar was predominant, though pine and oak were also used in the construction of homes and other buildings. The lumber was used for framing, siding, clapboards, shutters, and shingles. The present

Millstone (photo by Albert D. Horner)

sawmill was built by Joseph Wharton in 1882 on the foundation of an existing mill.

While the earlier sawmill was powered by a water wheel, the 1882 installation boasted a more efficient water-driven metal turbine. Power was transferred from the turbine to the mill's machinery by a series of belts and pulleys. The early saws were fitted with vertical blades and driven by a piston. After a log was fed into a carriage and locked in place, the blade was moved up and down to cut through it, much like an oversized two-man saw held upright. In later years a circular saw was installed at the mill.

Though much of the lumber was milled for use by the village, Batsto account books during the 1830s—when two sawmills were in operation—show that timber products such as shingling and planking were sold and shipped from Batsto Landing along with cordwood for use in furnaces and fireplaces. Later, during the years Wharton owned the property, the sawmill was clearly a commercial enterprise, with lumber sales in 1884 reaching almost $10,000 and producing a $5400 profit for Wharton. Soon after the state purchased the Batsto estate in the mid-1950s, the sawmill was restored in order to provide siding, shingles, beams, and other materials needed for the restoration and maintenance of the village buildings.

BLACKSMITH AND WHEELWRIGHT SHOPS

Integral to the running of any early American industrial village was the blacksmith shop. The blacksmith forged hand-made nails, hinges, tools, horseshoes, rims for wagon wheels, iron rings for barrels, and bolts and parts for all matter of equipment and machinery. Virtually every metal product in need of repair was taken to the smithy, and when there was no farrier in the village the blacksmith was often called on to shoe the village horses and oxen.

The present Batsto blacksmith shop is believed to have been built sometime before 1850; it was restored in the 1960s some years after the state purchased the property.

Next to the blacksmith shop is the wheelwright shop. Wheelwrights made wooden wheels for wagons and other vehicles of conveyance.

Interior of blacksmith shop (photo by Albert D. Horner)

The wheelwright also fixed the blacksmith's forged rim onto the wheel.

The blacksmith and wheelwright shops, originally separate structures, were moved to their present location during the Wharton years. Budd Wilson, historical archaeologist during the 1960s, believes that these buildings originally stood near the river to the west of the furnace.

THE FARM BUILDINGS

The range barn and pit silo were utilized as part of Joseph Wharton's cattle breeding venture. The attached pit silo was dug in the ground and covered over with a building. Grain was stored for the village animals in the pit silo. The sheep shed was located next to it.

The piggery was the hog slaughtering and pork processing establishment within the village. The adjoining brick tower holds a water storage tank on its third floor, and it is believed that water was pumped to the tower by a hydraulic ram as early as 1832. The water tank supplied water to the cast-iron cauldron used in the rendering

Piggery (center-left with tower) and other farm buildings
(courtesy of the New Jersey State Archives)

process and located in the piggery. The piggery water tank also provided water to various other barns on the property.

The carriage barn housed the village wagons, stages, and other
vehicles. Although the current building was rebuilt by Wharton, its
foundation dates to the Richards era. The Batsto stagecoach, which
sits in this barn with other horse-drawn wagons, is typical of wagons
used for overland transportation during the 19th century.

The stone stable, built in 1830, provided shelter for the work
horses. The horses used in the business and farm were kept separate
from the finer horses used by the family. Those horses were housed in
the barn next to where the carriages were kept.

The mule barn was constructed in 1852 of Jersey sandstone. The
building housed the town's mules and also served as a hay storeroom.

THE COMPANY STORE AND POST OFFICE

The company store was critical to all who made their livelihood at
Batsto. It was where villagers purchased whatever they could not

produce at home. Wages were paid in store credit, or scrip, and the workers and their families had accounts tied to their wages against which they could purchase goods at the store. The store sold cloth, bonnets, shoes, medicines, animal feed, tools, candles, soap, cheese, candy, coffee, tea, and spices. Sewing items like thread and trim, as well as an assortment of shovels, iron pots, and kettles were also available for sale.

In the town's heyday it is estimated that four to six ships a week made their way to Batsto laden with goods for the store. These same ships left the landing loaded with iron and glass products.

G. Edwin Brumbaugh, restoration architect, believed that the store was one of the oldest buildings in Batsto, possibly predating the original section of the mansion. It is believed that the store's oldest section, the eastern part of the structure, was built late in the 18th century. During those early years when the Richards family owned the property, the store was located on the upper level next to what is today the post office. The lower rooms were used for the storage and sale of products from the gristmill. The western brick end was added by Jesse Richards in 1846. The room on the upper level that now serves as the post office became the company office in 1847.

Company store (photo by Albert D. Horner)

When Wharton purchased the property, in order to direct traffic away from what had become the front door of the mansion, he moved the store to the lower level where it can be found today. The store's porch was also added during the Wharton era.

The Batsto post office, located on the building's upper level, is believed to be the oldest operating post office in New Jersey and the third oldest in the country using its original name, building, and location. This post office, which began operating in 1852, still cancels outgoing mail by hand. Due to its historical site status it was never assigned a zip code.

The post office was moved from Batsto to Pleasant Mills in 1870 following the decline of the glass industry. After Wharton purchased the property the post office was reopened in 1882. It closed in 1911 when both the Pleasant Mills and Batsto offices were replaced with a rural delivery route. In 1966, after the purchase by the state, the post office was reopened.

WORKERS' HOMES

The Batsto Rent Roll books—account books maintained by Robert Stewart during his tenure as the company bookkeeper, and later as manager—tell us there were at least 77 houses in Batsto Village from 1846 to 1874. These homes were scattered over six streets including Bridge Street, which was the main road through town. There were 32 houses on Bridge Street during the glass years; after the 1874 fire only 14 remained. These houses, which were rebuilt by the state in the 1960s, are still standing today.

At one time there were at least 20 and as many as 24 homes on Water Street, which runs along the western side of the pond, but today only one double house remains; it is utilized as the nature center. There were once six houses on Oak Street, but the fire left only three standing, along with another five each on Tuckaho and Broad. On Canal Street, which ran southeast of the gristmill, at one time there were eight houses. Today there are none.

The most common type of worker's home was a two-story, single frame house. Originally these homes had a cooking/sitting room, a small parlor or bedroom depending on the needs of the family, and

Drawing by Jack Cresson

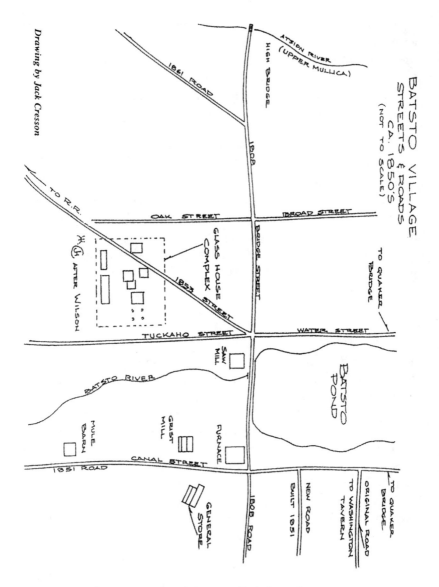

BATSTO VILLAGE
STREETS & ROADS
CA. 1850'S
(NOT TO SCALE)

1850s Batsto Village streets and roads (courtesy of Jack Cresson)

Bridge Street workers' homes (photo by Albert D. Horner)

two small bedrooms on the second floor. Each of the homes had a lean-to kitchen shed at the back. These kitchens were attached to the original homes in the 1850s. There were also 12 two-story double houses (six structures). Two of these, the two end houses, still exist on Bridge Street today. All the houses on Oak Street were two-story, single frame dwellings, of which three remain. At one time there were also 11 single-story frame houses and at least one log house at Batsto. None of these homes exist today.

As you walk through Batsto Village today, experiencing the bucolic setting of a bygone era, it is easy to see why Joseph Wharton hung on to the estate even after most of his Pine Barrens money-making operations had failed. Although he only occasionally visited his Batsto estate, perhaps it reminded him of the road he had not taken, or of the path he pursued when just a young man, bringing to mind the simpler years of his youth and imagination.

Restoration

By the mid-1970s Batsto was once more a village brimming with life. Hundreds of visitors flocked to the site weekly to enjoy its cultural as well as natural resources. From the clippity-clop of horses' hooves to the buzz of the sawmill to the hammering of the blacksmith's tools, sounds of a bustling village filled the air. Attractions included guided tours of the newly refurnished mansion and demonstrations at the fully operable grist- and sawmills and recently refitted blacksmith shop. Many of the workers' homes, which had been restored and furnished as they would have appeared in the 1850s, were staffed by talented craftsmen demonstrating candle making, weaving, chair caning, wood carving, and pottery making. A naturalist was on hand to lead informative walks on well-designed nature trails that wove through bogs, sandy beaches, and woodlands. The nature center housed exhibits showcasing the flora and fauna of the region.

Farm animals meandered around pastures near the mansion, and, for a few cents, children could purchase a handful of corn to coax the village critters to nibble from their palms. The company store, where refreshments could be purchased, was outfitted to look as it had appeared in the 19th century. Class trips from every section of the state brought thousands of students to the newly opened historic site. Picnic tables were filled with families relaxing in the peaceful atmosphere of the village. Artists and photographers were frequently spotted throughout the grounds attempting to capture on canvas and film the beauty of the rustic setting.

The Batsto stagecoach, which made a round trip through the village every 15 minutes, was one of the restored site's most popular attractions. The stage, believed to have been built in the 1850s, was thought to have originally been used on the run between Cooper's Ferry (Camden) and Leed's Point.

During the summer months the stagecoach ride, which cost 35 cents a trip, operated from 10 AM to 6 PM. In those years Batsto Village had an estimated 200,000 visitors annually.

STATE PURCHASE OF WHARTON TRACT

When the state purchased the Wharton Tract in the mid-1950s most of the village structures at Batsto were in need of repair, with the exception of the mansion which was in fairly good condition. Many of the buildings needed roofs, and most were structurally unsound due to rot and decay. The dam had washed out in 1951 during a hurricane, so the lake was down, and both the gristmill and sawmill were inoperable.

Subsequent to the state purchase most of the 18 homes in the village were leased to private residents. One of the stipulations when the state bought the Wharton lands was that people already living in the village would have a lifetime right to stay in their homes. After

Batsto stagecoach (courtesy of the New Jersey State Archives)

the state purchase some families left but at least half of the houses remained occupied. Vera and Percy Adams stayed on for years. Percy served as a seasonal guide after his retirement from the Burlington County Highway Department. He died in 1976 in the same house where he'd been born in 1904. Vera stayed on until 1989 and was the last of the original residents to live in the village.

Another couple, Carrie and Charles Mick, lived in the west end of the village. After Charles died Carrie cleaned the visitor center until the state said she had to retire because she was 70 years old, the state's mandatory retirement age. Maurice Mick, Carrie and Charles's son, had grown up in the village and stayed on as well. In the mid-1950s Maurice was hired as a watchman and later as the stagecoach driver. Adeline Pepper, a writer and author of the *Glass Gaffers of New Jersey* lived there, too. In her free time she worked as a volunteer excavating near the iron furnace. Annie Carter, Batsto naturalist, lived in the house once occupied by Wharton's farm manager Alonzo Norton, on a knoll on the east side of lake. She turned the downstairs of her home into a museum and lived upstairs.

WHARTON SUB-COMMITTEE

After the purchase, the state immediately began surveying the tract. A sub-committee, with members from a number of state agencies and disciplines, was formed to produce a plan that would provide for multiple uses of the newly purchased public lands. The first meeting of the Wharton Sub-Committee was held on May 28, 1956, and a report with the committee's recommendations was approved on June 13, 1956. The historic sites component of the committee recommended initiating research, including archaeology, to establish historical facts about sites within the tract. It also recommended that Batsto be operated as an historic village and be opened to the public immediately.

In late 1956 an advisory group called the Batsto Citizens Advisory Committee (BCAC) was formed. Later this group would be referred to as the Batsto Citizens Committee (BCC). The group was initially created to advise and assist in the restoration of Historic Batsto Village and to promote the region's rich historical heritage. The

BCAC consisted of 36 individuals appointed by the Commissioner of the Department of Conservation and Economic Development—the predecessor of the Department of Environmental Protection. The individuals were chosen for their specific knowledge in many aspects of history, archaeology, architecture, metallurgy, museum management, law, antiques, etc. They were considered experts and among them were a number of Pine Barrens authors including Henry Charlton Beck, Arthur Pierce, Henry Bisbee, Jack Boucher, and William McMahon. Their purpose was to help the citizens of New Jersey preserve and develop Wharton State Forest and Batsto Village. At the time the state had few staff to handle the preservation and interpretation of historic sites and looked to BCAC to provide such support for the Wharton Lands.

Charles Kier, Batsto Citizen Committee member and amateur archaeologist working under the direction of Dr. Dorothy Cross, New Jersey State archaeologist, was the first to document seasonal prehistoric sites at Batsto. Also during this period, Captain and Mrs. Charles I. Wilson, longtime friends of Batsto Village, were the first to conduct exploratory probes of the Batsto furnace site. Later, in 1957, Roland Robbins initiated work on the gristmill and iron furnace site.

J. Albert Starkey was hired in 1958 and served as the principal archaeologist at Batsto until 1963. Budd Wilson and several others worked under Starkey's direction. Excavations included an ore boat which had been found in the drained lake, the furnace site, the lime kiln, the area where the bog ore and charcoal were stored and a few slag heaps. The ore boat, which was believed to be about 150 years old at the time of the excavation, was a shallow draft boat built to haul bog ore to the furnace complex. The boat was removed from the lake during the summer of 1958 prior to the dam being repaired and the lake re-flooded. Starkey also did an investigation of a house foundation found on the west terrace of the mansion property, determining that its construction dated to prerevolutionary times.

The Wharton Sub-Committee report also recommended the hiring of a restoration architect to do a study of the historic sites within the tract. Joseph Truncer, who would later become the director of the Division of Parks and Forestry within the New Jersey

Iron furnace excavation (photo courtesy of Budd Wilson)

Department of Conservation and Economic Development, led the initiative and is considered to be the "architect" of the restoration efforts at Batsto Village.

RESTORATION ARCHITECT HIRED
AND THE WORK BEGINS

In 1959, restoration architect G. Edwin Brumbaugh, who had done work at Fort Mifflin and the Old Swedes Church in Philadelphia, was hired to do a study of the Wharton tract and provide recommendations for its restoration and interpretation. Brumbaugh's report, which was structured on *The Interpretation Philosophy of Colonial Williamsburg*, written by Dr. Edward Alexander in 1957, was completed in 1960. *Historical Aspects of the Wharton Tract* recommended the return of Batsto Village to its historically significant industrial era of the 1840s–1850s, the years when both the iron furnace and glassworks were operating, and during which Jesse Richards managed Batsto. Brumbaugh wanted the Batsto restoration to recreate an early industrial settlement in the wilderness, representing an authentic picture of life in the New Jersey Pine Barrens back when industries had supported the community. He advocated that all traces of Joseph Wharton be erased, including his 1878 restoration of the mansion. Brumbaugh felt that Wharton, who had torn down the glass house and dug out a carp pond at the furnace site, had employed drastic measures to obliterate all traces of historic industrial activity, thereby making restoration efforts difficult.

Brumbaugh's report referenced 36 surviving structures at Batsto that he felt should be restored and preserved. Additionally he recommended the reconstruction of the iron furnace, the glassworks, and the stamping, rolling, and slitting mills. He stated that prior to this reconstruction major archaeological work must be done on the grounds of the iron furnace and glass house. "This is the only possible course if the historic furnace is to be restored and the entire historical display is to be consistent," he said, adding, "The Victorian remodeling of Joseph Wharton has nothing to do with the significant history of Batsto." Brumbaugh recommended the building of a visitor center to include a museum, information desk, gift shop, library, and auditorium.

Apart from the Batsto Village restorations, Brumbaugh proposed the restoration of the Atsion mansion, company store, cotton mill, church, Etheridge house (manager's home), workers' homes, and schoolhouse. He also advocated that historical exhibits and a marine museum be built at Crowley's and Abe Nichol's Landings to memorialize the privateering efforts of the patriots during the American Revolution. Unfortunately for us, other than the restoration of the Atsion mansion and company store none of these recommendations was realized.

Brumbaugh's plan was approved in 1960 and a few years later he was retained by the state to supervise the restoration. Though Batsto was open to the public, relatively little restoration work was undertaken during the first few years, although the blacksmith shop was outfitted and made operational. The first Batsto visitor center was built and dedicated by Governor Richard Hughes on May 15, 1964. The center was basic and included an information desk, souvenir shop, restrooms, and a library. In 1983, the Center was greatly enlarged. The new addition included a museum with exhibits focusing on nine phases of the Pine Barrens and its early uses, from Native Americans to iron and glass, as well as the post-Wharton era. A later addition to the center occurred in 2005.

In order to provide the shingles, structural lumber, and siding needed to restore the village structures, the sawmill went through an extensive restoration from 1963 to 1965. In the early 1960s, a restored stagecoach began operating at Batsto. A fully functioning post office was reopened in 1962. By June 1966 the store and post office had been restored and were open to the public. In 1967 the gristmill was restored. The following two years saw a focus on the farm complex, including the threshing barn, stable, range barn, and piggery. By the late 1960s work had started on the village houses. An estimated 60–70 percent of materials utilized in restoration of village buildings were supplied by the Batsto sawmill. The range barn alone used 50,000 roof shingles.

Blacksmith bellows (photo courtesy of the New Jersey State Archives)

Original visitor center (photo courtesy of Budd Wilson)

On September 11, 1970 the Batsto Historic District was placed on the New Jersey Register of Historic Places. It was placed on the National Register of Historic Places on September 10, 1971.

The natural beauty and unique ecology of the site was not ignored, and in 1960 the Pine Barrens Conservationists, an early environmental group, conceived of the idea of creating the Batsto Nature Area. A nature trail, completed under the guidance and direction of J. Albert Starkey, featured 150 species of native plants and flowers. The trail meandered over five bridges, around bogs and swamps, and through scrub forests and sandy beaches. Much of the trail was located at the confluence of the Atsion (now referred to as the Mullica) and Meschescatauxin Rivers and was on the bottom of an old mill pond which had been drained after its dam blew out in the mid-1920s. Guided tours of the trail were run daily, while trail markers and signs provided information for visitors wanting to go it alone. A booklet, *Ferns, Plants and Shrubs of the Wharton Tract*, which listed 400 plants of the region as well as a trail map—prepared by Louis and Eileen Hand, members of the Pine Barrens Conservationists—was available for purchase at the visitor center.

Glassworks excavation (photo courtesy of Budd Wilson)

Indian artifact (chert blade) found during the glassworks excavation (photo courtesy of Budd Wilson)

Annie Carter, Batsto's first naturalist, created a nature center on the east side of the lake to house exhibits relating to the ecology of the New Jersey Pine Barrens.

LATER ARCHAEOLOGY

From 1965 through 1967, historical archaeologist Budd Wilson directed an excavation of the glassworks complex that included two melting furnaces, the flattening house, cutting house, pot house, lime and wood sheds. During the excavation Wilson discovered several

Native American artifacts estimated to be as much as 3,500 years old, indicating that Archaic Indians once used the area as a seasonal hunting site.

On July 10, 1978, the Batsto Archaeological Lab and Office, located in the woods off of Rt. 563 in Green Bank, was leveled by a fire, which destroyed several thousand artifacts including maps, documents, and drawings. The lab and office, which had been surrounded by a six-foot fence, appeared to have been ransacked prior to the fire, suggesting that the blaze had been set by arsonists. Most of the artifacts lost in the fire had been excavated at the Batsto iron furnace and glassworks sites. The salvaged items represented less than 10 percent of what had been stored there. Countless hours had been spent excavating, cleaning, identifying, evaluating, and cataloguing the stored artifacts lost in the fire, and the loss was immeasurable. After salvage efforts were completed the site was bulldozed.

From 1983 to 1993 further archaeological work was conducted by the Batsto Citizens Committee under the supervision of Jack Cresson, Chairman of the BCC Archaeology Committee. Cresson also did archaeological work in the mid-1980s at the mansion site to determine construction episodes.

BATSTO CITIZENS COMMITTEE

The Batsto Citizens Committee initially had many functions and was involved in all aspects of the restoration of the village. The group took a strong interest in the preservation and archaeology of the site and made it a priority to obtain artifacts and records relating to its history. With the assistance of the Atlantic County Historical Society, the BCC organized a fund drive to assist in furnishing the mansion.

The BCC also published booklets concerning Batsto and Wharton State Forest, including Jack Boucher's *Of Batsto and Bog Iron* and Franklin Kemp's *A Nest of Rebel Pirates*. The committee published a quarterly newspaper, the *Batsto Citizens Gazette*, focusing on the history not only of Batsto but of surrounding and related areas. Members did excellent research and wrote well-documented articles that added to the knowledge of the site and the region. The BCC sponsored many popular events at Batsto including the Decoy and

Woodcarver show, the Historic Arts and Crafts festival, and the Country Living Fair.

BCC sponsored and hosted two special homecoming events, first for Wharton family descendants in 1980 and then for the Richards family in the fall of 1984. A Friends of Batsto group was established for those who wanted to support BCC activities through donations, with a subscription to the *Batsto Citizens Gazette* provided as a benefit of membership.

The BCC, originally needed for its expertise and advisory role, changed its mission when the state hired staff to oversee and manage the historical aspects of the village. When the group found its original responsibilities being turned over to state personnel, it had to define a new role for itself. During this transition period the members of BCC decided to create a separate nonprofit corporation. In 1997 BCC became the Batsto Citizens Committee Incorporated (BCCI) and has since operated as an independent support organization with a mission statement parallel to that of the state.

With a decline in the demand for archaeological and historical research, BCCI turned to other aspects of its mission. The group is currently focused on the promotion of Batsto Village, seeking to raise public awareness of its historical significance as well as of its unique ecological surrounds. BCCI continues its fundraising efforts in support of special projects and the operational needs of the Parks and Forestry staff, which includes running the annual Country Living Fair and other historically-themed events.

BATSTO VILLAGE PLAN

In 1993, an initiative undertaken by the Division of Parks and Forestry assessed the current state of the Batsto site for the purpose of further development of the village. The purpose of the initiative was "....to design an overall coherent development of Batsto Village as a living history museum." The Batsto Village Plan outlined and analyzed the existing conditions of the site and provided a blueprint for future restoration, interpretation, and capital improvement.

Batsto Country Living Fair (photo by Albert D. Horner)

The state's report reviewed work previously proposed or completed at the village including G. Edwin Brumbaugh's recommendations that the iron furnace complex and glassworks be reconstructed and all traces of the Wharton era erased. They noted that although these initiatives had not been undertaken, many of Brumbaugh's other proposals had been accomplished. By the late 1970s most of the structures in the village—including the gristmill, sawmill, and company store—had been fully restored as recommended by Brumbaugh. The archaeological work he had proposed had also been completed.

In direct conflict with Brumbaugh's vision, the Batsto Village Plan recommended the Wharton era as the major focus of the future interpretive program at Batsto. It noted in its rationale that the current physical plant reflected the changes made by Joseph Wharton and stated that most of the existing structures within the village reflected that era. It was thus the plan of the division to interpret Batsto Village as a 19th-century farm, while depicting its earlier history through interpretive media such as artifacts, indoor exhibits, literature, and self-guided tours. The plan stated that the iron/glass industrial complexes reconstruction recommended by Brumbaugh could not be realized due to federal regulations, state building codes, lack of historical documentation, and insufficient funding.

The BCC reacted strongly against the plan, arguing forcefully that Batsto's Wharton era was not as historically significant as its earlier industrial period. The committee felt that to concentrate on such a short time span would distort the true history of the village. Though the division report stated that most of the structures reflected the agricultural and commercial enterprises of Wharton, BCC countered that 90 percent of the structures in the village dated from the industrial period of the Richards family. It contended that only five dated from the Wharton era, including the sawmill, carriage house, one of the workers' homes (the Alonzo Norton house), the engine house, and mansion restoration.

After a period of contentious debate the state initiated a dispute resolution process to resolve the differing viewpoints of the BCC and Division of Parks and Forestry staff. A series of seven mediation meetings, beginning in November 1995 and running through September 1996, brought the two sides to the table. After long hours of debate the participants reached consensus. The resultant revised plan included the following highlights, as reported in the Fall-Winter 1996 edition of the *Batsto Citizens Gazette*:

1) Batsto's 101 industrial years would be interpreted not just in the museum setting but also through wayside exhibits on the village grounds at the archaeological sites of iron and glass production.

2) Relocation of the ore boat, bog ore, and charcoal exhibit to a location near the original furnace site.

3) Additions to the plan for interpretation to include: a) European settlement 1707 to 1764 of the environs of Batsto; b) the burning of Chestnut Neck (privateering port on the Mullica) and the failed plan of the British to destroy the Batsto Ironworks; and c) emphasis on the unique Pine Barrens culture and lifestyle with focus on

the Miller-Coleman family whose members had lived and worked at Batsto for eight decades.

4) Information about all of Batsto's history would be sought from every viable source rather than research focused mainly on the Wharton era 1876–1909.

With the continuing cooperation, commitment, and dedication of the State of New Jersey, the Batsto Citizens Committee, and countless others, Batsto Village is today a significant and authentically interpreted historic site visited by tens of thousands of people annually. Village structures continue to be restored and upgraded, as volunteers and state employees work together to bring the history of Batsto Village alive for its many visitors. New events and projects continue to be proposed, planned, and carried out, making Batsto Village a premier historic destination within the state of New Jersey.

Atsion: Sister Village

The fortunes of Batsto and Atsion were entwined from the beginning. In 1765 Charles Read constructed a forge by a river that the local native people referred to as the Atsayunk. Read, who was simultaneously building three other ironworks, planned to convert the pig iron manufactured at Batsto into a more durable product at his forge on the Atsion River, later known as the Mullica. Daily ox carts pulled heavy loads of pig iron to the forge to be hammered into bar iron, Atsion's principal product during the Read years. The finished iron was then returned over the same dirt roads to be shipped out at Batsto Landing at The Forks of the Little Egg Harbor (Mullica) River to markets up and down the East Coast.

In 1774, when Read was no longer a proprietor of both ironworks, new owners built a furnace at Atsion to allow them to reduce their own iron from ore and become independent of Batsto. But once again the two villages were linked—this time by contentious court battles over timber, water, and ore rights that went on for years.

When Samuel Richards purchased Atsion in 1819, Batsto was already owned by the Richards family and relations between the two ironworks were once again amiable and mutually cooperative. During the later period when Joseph Wharton and his heirs owned Atsion and Batsto—from the late 1800s until the mid-1950s—both villages were considered part of the Wharton farm and operated in support of one another.

When the state purchased the Wharton tract in the mid-1950s, its early plans included the reconstruction of both villages. A plan to operate a stage coach between Batsto and Atsion, following the same route traveled by the early ox carts, was once proposed by state officials though this never came to pass.

Today, Atsion is a gateway into Wharton State Forest as well as a popular recreational center for those interested in enjoying its beautiful lake, hiking trails, and camping and picnicking facilities.

THE EARLY YEARS

Charles Read, a man so prominent in New Jersey colonial politics he was once second in command to the governor, was the first to realize the potential for manufacturing iron from bog ore in the state's southern pine woods. Read, whose story is covered in some detail in Chapter 1, knew the area contained large stores of high-grade bog ore, plentiful water, and vast stands of pine wood—critical elements in the production of bog iron.

In 1765 Read constructed a string of ironworks in the New Jersey Pine Barrens. He built iron furnaces at Batsto, Aetna (at the time, Etna), and Taunton, and a forge at Atsion. Finding himself cash-strapped, he took on two partners at Atsion: David Ogden—who with Read was a member of the governor's council—and Lawrence Salter, a businessman from Burlington County. The agreement gave the two new partners a quarter share each (Salter was slightly less than a quarter at 249/1000) and left Read with the controlling interest.

The furnace flourished, but Read, over-extended financially and in poor health, advertised his share for sale in the *Pennsylvania Journal* in October 1770. It wasn't until March 1773 that he finally sold his share to two associates, Abel James and Henry Drinker, prominent Philadelphia Quakers who were business partners in a shipping and importing firm.

On the eve of selling Atsion, Read turned over all of his remaining assets to trustees and left the country in an attempt to settle his recently deceased wife's estate on Antigua. He died in obscurity one year later in North Carolina where he had set up a small shop.

On April 2, 1773, David Ogden sold his quarter interest to Salter who now owned 499/1000. On April 6, 1773, the three remaining partners purchased the adjoining Goshen Sawmill tract and an additional 1000 acres of woodland became part of the Atsion Forge property. A journal maintained by Henry Drinker's wife, Elizabeth, tells a story of riding horseback with her husband from Philadelphia to visit the ironworks (for the first time in 15 years). Elizabeth writes about stopping off in Moorestown where they spent the night, then after borrowing a wagon, continuing on their journey. Ten miles into their travel the couple reached Medford Lakes where they stopped to visit the Aetna Furnace operated by Charles Read IV, the son of Charles Read. After another ten miles the Drinkers arrived at Atsion at the home of Dolly and Lawrence Salter, who had remained as the ironworks manager. Later that day Elizabeth and Dolly rode three miles to the Goshen Sawmill property to bring dinner to their husbands, who were surveying the new land.

One year later the three partners built a furnace at Atsion. No longer dependent on Batso for ore, they dug their own from the pond bed when the furnace shut down each winter and the lake was drained. Ore was also dug three or four miles above the ironworks then boated down river on barges.

In late 1774 John Cox, then owner of Batsto, sued Atsion over timber rights and the use of the Atsion River. Though it would take years to resolve, the lawsuit was finally settled by arbitration in 1793. Atsion was awarded timber rights on certain tracts, and Batsto was given ore rights on others. Both were given free use of the Atsion River.

Another later lawsuit between the two entities occurred in 1786 when Atsion management dug a canal between the Meschescatauxin Creek and Atsion River to increase the flow of water over the Atsion dam. This action flooded the ore beds below the dam when flood gates were opened, forcing Batsto ore diggers to stop work. This lawsuit took over seven years to resolve.

With the onset of the Revolutionary War, Henry Drinker, whose Quaker beliefs led him to oppose the war, shut down the Atsion Furnace. Salter, however, continued to operate the forge and during the conflict was given a contract to furnish evaporating pans to a saltworks in Toms River. In 1776 the ironworks was contracted to supply ships of the Pennsylvania Navy with iron products. Whether these products were munitions or other items such as chains, anchors, or spikes is not known.

After the Revolution the ironworks was back in business and for a number of years Atsion prospered. By the turn of the century three sawmills and a gristmill were operating at Atsion. Two wharves located in Lumberton on the Rancocas River provided a direct route to ship finished products to Philadelphia after they were carted overland from the ironworks. Products going to the New York markets continued to be shipped from the Forks of the Little Egg Harbor River. During the post-Revolutionary War years, tons of pig iron, bar iron, stoves, kettles, and plowshares were being made at the ironworks. It is believed by historians that the original Franklin stoves in Congress Hall, which served as the Congress of the United States between 1790 and 1800, were forged at Atsion.

When Lawrence Salter died in 1783, he left his heirs slightly less than a half interest in the ironworks. The next year Abel James declared bankruptcy and Henry Drinker bought his share of Atsion, leaving Drinker and the Salter heirs in full possession of the ironworks.

In October 1794 the furnace burned down, causing many days of lost production and a large expense to get the ironworks rebuilt. The Salter heirs and Henry Drinker were increasingly at odds over the management of the ironworks. In one incident William Salter— Lawrence's son and heir—took the store keys by force from a manager appointed by Henry Drinker. In another dispute, a scow with 26 tons of Atsion iron that had shipped from the Lumberton wharf went missing. When Henry Drinker went looking for the scow he found that it had been sunk in a storm. Drinker also discovered that John Salter—another son and heir of Lawrence Salter—had asked a local sheriff to provide security for the scow and its cargo. Elizabeth Drinker, writing in her journal, noted that the Salter family "had hidden it on its way down river, lest H.D. (Henry Drinker) seize it and the storm, in some measure, settled the matter."

The disputes between the two parties continued, and, though no records exist to explain what transpired, we do know that the ironworks was put on the auction block at Philadelphia's Merchant Coffee House in 1805. Jacob Downing, Drinker's son-in-law, bought the entire estate including those shares belonging to his father-in-law and, by order of the court, those belonging to the heirs of Lawrence Salter. Henry Drinker, however, may have acted as the behind-the-scenes financier in this deal as later records show that he continued as half owner with his son-in-law.

For a number of years Downing prospered, but by 1817 he was in financial trouble, having defaulted on a mortgage he had taken on part of the Atsion estate. On June 5, 1819, the Bank of North America sold Downing's half share to Samuel Richards, eldest son of William Richards, ironmaster at Batsto. By this time, Samuel already owned two other iron furnaces at Weymouth and Martha.

Richards kept the Atsion Ironworks operating for the next six months making water pipes for the city of Philadelphia. When the Philadelphia contract was fulfilled, he put Atsion up for sale. Overnight, Atsion became a ghost town.

SAMUEL RICHARDS

Samuel Richards was born on May 8, 1769, somewhere near the Warwick Furnace where his father was then employed. In 1784, when Samuel was 15, his father acquired the Batsto Ironworks, and it was here that Samuel learned about iron making. By the time Samuel was 27 he was representing his father's firm in Philadelphia. In 1796 he purchased Pleasant Mills, a mill complex near Batsto. Though the complex was originally a sawmill site, Samuel and a partner established a mill for reclaiming wool from used garments. By 1804 the business was in trouble, and there is no further mention of it after 1805.

Samuel would become the only one of William's children to surpass his father's success. In addition to Atsion, his Weymouth and Martha Ironworks were successful operations. He would later purchase the Speedwell Furnace, though this ironworks would not meet with the same success as his others.

On November 18, 1797, Samuel married a young widow, Mary Smith Morgan, whose father was a wealthy Philadelphia shipping magnate. After marrying, the couple moved to Water Street to be near the family store, located in the heart of the city's waterfront district. By the turn of the century four children would be born to

Samuel Richards (courtesy of the New Jersey State Archives)

Samuel and Mary. Sadly, by 1803 all four had perished in a yellow fever epidemic that was devastating Philadelphia, particularly in the area near the wharves where the Richards lived.

In 1802, Samuel and his cousin Joseph Ball purchased the White Clay Creek Mills in Delaware, a large grist- and sawmill complex. Samuel's father-in-law was included in the transaction.

During these years Samuel also owned shares in the Eagle Ironworks in Philadelphia.

In the early 1800s the family moved to 357 Mulberry Street (now Arch), a good distance from the waterfront. In the following ten years four more children would be born to Mary and Samuel though only three would survive to adulthood. In 1820, after 23 years of marriage to Samuel, Mary Richards, who was just 50 years old, passed away at her home on Mulberry Street.

On October 8, 1822, Samuel married Anna Maria Martin Witherspoon, the widow of a wealthy New Yorker. Samuel was 53 and Maria, as she was called by her family, was 39. The couple, who resided at Ninth and Arch, went on to have three children together though one would die in infancy.

REVITALIZATION OF ATSION

Samuel Richards bought out Henry Drinker's one-half share of Atsion in 1824 and reestablished the ironworks and village. Once more the Atsion forge, furnace, gristmill, and sawmills were operating at full steam. Under the capable management of Samuel Richards, an experienced ironmaster, the years that followed would be the most prosperous in Atsion's history. During this period, from 1824 through 1842, the year of Samuel's death, 100 men were employed in the village and 600 to 700 people were dependent on the works for their subsistence. The main product manufactured was stoves, though Atsion also made and sold kettles, window grates, pipes, and bridge castings as well as pig and bar iron. The furnace was producing 800–900 tons of castings and forged products and 150–200 tons of bar iron annually. The schooner *Atsion* was regularly loaded with finished iron products, sailing from Batsto Landing to markets up and down the East Coast.

In 1826 the Richards built an elegant mansion at Atsion in the rural Greek Revival style of architecture, which was popular at the time. Though the family's main residence was in Philadelphia, after the Atsion mansion was built they often spent the warmer months at the village. During the Richards era many large social functions took place in the mansion. Descending from carriages on the north side of the house, guests would be ushered into a wide hallway that connected with two well-proportioned parlors on one side and a spacious dining room on the other. Though there was a warming kitchen on the main floor, the main kitchen was located in the basement. Family bedchambers were located on the second floor, and four smaller bedrooms for servants were located on the third floor. There were many happy occasions celebrated in this home, including the birth of Maria Richards in 1826 and, two years later, the birth of her brother, William Henry Richards.

Atsion, like Batsto, was a company town where the workers were paid in scrip that could only be used at the store owned by the iron-master. As with any company town, the Atsion company store—built by Samuel Richards in 1827—was the place where village folk gathered to hear the news of the day and to purchase all the basic necessities. The Atsion store sold food, farm tools and equipment, animal grain, medicine, cloth, and sewing supplies. For many years it also housed a post office.

In 1828 Samuel Richards built a small clapboard church a short distance east of the mansion. Shortly after the church's construction

Atsion mansion (photo by Albert D. Horner)

Atsion church (photo by Albert D. Horner)

Samuel deeded it and the adjacent burial ground to a group of trustees to be used by "all religious denominations professing Christian religion."

The ironworks and village prospered until Samuel's death in 1842 at age 73. After providing amply for his widow, Maria, Samuel's will divided his Weymouth property between daughters Elizabeth Ann and Sarah, from his first marriage, and his Atsion property between Maria and William Henry, his two children by Maria. (Samuel's son Thomas, from his marriage to Mary, had died in 1839.) At the time of Samuel's passing the Atsion property included 128,000 acres. William Henry would receive the south end and Maria the north end, which included the ironworks and village.

MARIA AND WILLIAM HENRY RICHARDS

Seven years after Samuel Richard's death, his daughter Maria married William Walton Fleming, whom she had met the year before during a soirée at her half-sister Sarah Colwell's home in Weymouth. At the time of their meeting, Walton, as he was known, was 31 years old and already considered a man of means. He owned the W.W. Fleming Cobalt and Nickel Works in Camden, as well as property in Philadelphia where he lived. When the couple married they moved to Atsion but also maintained a home in Philadelphia. Walton, who had been welcomed into all the Richards's other enterprises including the organization of the Camden and Atlantic Railroad, took over management of the ironworks. But by now a richer ore and a more efficient fuel in the form of coal had been discovered in Pennsylvania, and the Pine Barrens iron industry was in sharp decline. Not long after Maria and Walton's marriage the Atsion Furnace went out of blast for the last time.

In 1852 Walton built a paper mill near the former site of the furnace. Historians believe that if this mill operated it wasn't for long, because in September 1854 Walton Fleming disappeared. No one, including his wife, knew where he had gone, but Maria soon learned that her husband was half a million dollars in debt, with much of that amount owed to his father, who had filed criminal charges against him.

Though it would take a year, Maria paid off Walton's debts and tracked down her husband in Brussels, Belgium. The couple reconciled and together with their son Samuel, Maria's mother, and niece in tow the family settled in Brussels, where they would live for the rest of their lives. It was fortunate that Maria and her mother had plenty of money, as from that time forward Walton never worked again but rather devoted himself to the arts, writing poetry and collecting art.

William Henry Richards, Maria's younger brother, had little interest in business and was considered a nonconformist by the family. With his father's wealth he was able to live the life he chose without having to worry about making a living. For a time William owned a tavern on Quaker Bridge Road, and later he lived on a 150-acre gentleman's farm on Atsion Road near Medford. Though there was some question regarding William Henry's marital status—the family clearly had its doubts—he lived for a time with Mary Thorne, with whom he had a daughter. In his will he left one-half of his estate to his "reputed" daughter, a quarter to his "reputed" wife, and a quarter to his sister, Maria. In spite of his use of the word "reputed" in regard to his wife and daughter, Atsion records show that he did, indeed, marry Mary Thorne on April 29, 1850, and that some years later Mary signed a deed as his wife. Their "reputed" daughter, Anna Maria Richards, lived with her grandmother—Samuel Richard's widow, for whom she had been named—from the time she was 2 years old; when Maria Richards Fleming moved her family to Belgium, Anna went with them.

FRUITLAND

Maria's share of the Atsion property was sold on April 13, 1861 to Jarvis Mason, who one year later sold it to Colonel William Patterson. Patterson purchased the property for $82,500 though he took a $60,000 mortgage for five years. Patterson hoped to establish a new community at Atsion based on agriculture. He called his company the Fruitland Improvement Company and changed the name of the town to Fruitland. By now the Raritan and Delaware Bay Railroad had built a line through the town, which Patterson hoped would provide an incentive to those interested in selling farm produce to the New York and Philadelphia markets.

As a first step Patterson made extravagant plans to grow sugar beets on a commercial scale. He invested $13,000 in a steam cable plough which had the capacity to plow 10 times more ground in one day than 20 five-plough-horse teams.

The land Patterson wasn't personally farming was divided into 25-acre farm plots. Though he managed to sell some of the lots, he had seriously over-extended himself, and his estate was liquidated for payment of debts in 1871. At the time, the Atsion estate included a mansion, store, four barns, 12 tenant homes, a gristmill, a paper mill (without any fixtures or machinery), and two sawmills.

ATSION GETS A NEW LEASE ON LIFE

On May 10, 1871, the Atsion estate was sold at masters sale for $48,200 to Maurice Raleigh, a wealthy Philadelphian. Raleigh, who changed the name of the town back to Atsion, enlarged the paper mill and turned it into a cotton mill. Cotton was brought in by rail, and the plant was soon turning out 500 pounds of cotton yarn a week.

Atsion cotton mill (photo courtesy of Budd Wilson)

At its height, during the mid-1870s, the mill employed as many as 170 workers.

Raleigh's mill was profitable, and it revitalized the town. He reopened the store, and in 1872—the same year public education came into effect in New Jersey—built a one-room schoolhouse for the children of the village. The school provided education for students from grades 1 through 5. The teacher, who taught all grades and subjects, made $20 a month and boarded with the families of her students. Raleigh also built carpenter and blacksmith shops. Atsion was in a boom period by 1880, with a population of 300.

When Maurice Raleigh died on January 10, 1882, his heirs, who first shut down the cotton mill, formed the Raleigh Land and Improvement Company and changed the name of the town to Raleigh. The family had plans to once more subdivide the property and establish a planned community. Advertisements claimed "…fertile farm land at $25 an acre, pure air, good water and absolute freedom from malaria." The Raleigh Land and Improvement Company lingered on for several years, but few lots were sold. In 1892 Joseph

Wharton bought the Atsion property, adding to his vast holdings in the New Jersey Pine Barrens.

THE WHARTON YEARS AT ATSION

When Wharton's plan to sell the water of the Pine Barrens to the cities of Philadelphia and Camden failed, he turned to farming. Bogs originally dug out for ore were planted with cranberries, and Raleigh's cotton mill was turned into a cranberry packing and sorting house. Shortly after purchasing the Atsion tract, Wharton hired Andrew Etheridge as his farm manager. Etheridge, as one of his caretaker responsibilities, managed the company store with help from his daughter Mayme, who also performed bookkeeping duties.

For a time peanuts were grown at Atsion in a field between the church and railroad. The Atsion icehouse, a huge building on the south side of the lake, was also a source of income for the estate. In winter, when the pond froze to a sufficient thickness, large square blocks of ice were cut from the lake. The blocks were stored between

Wharton-era concrete barn (photo courtesy of Budd Wilson)

layers of sawdust in the icehouse and sold during the summer months prior to the advent of refrigeration. Log cabins on the north side of the lake were rented out to summer visitors as they are today.

When Etheridge died in 1925 his son-in-law, Leeson Small, became the Atsion caretaker. Mayme continued to maintain the books and operate the store.

After the state purchased the property in 1955, Atsion became a recreation area offering camping, bathing, picnicking, fishing, and

Etheridge house (photo courtesy of Budd Wilson)

boating. In 1977 the state built a recreation center that included bathhouse facilities, restrooms, and a food concession. Lifeguards manned the beach and lake during the summer season. All these facilities continue to be available at Atsion to this day.

The Atsion company store was restored in the mid-1960s and today serves as the Atsion Forest Office. From April through October, the office is open to visitors and provides information about cabin rentals and camping facilities located at the nearby Goshen and Atsion campgrounds. Each of the nine lakefront log cabins has a kitchen with an electric stove and refrigerator and bathrooms with hot and cold running water. All cabins have screened-in porches and outside picnic tables and grills as well as access to the lake for boating and fishing.

The Atsion mansion, long closed to the public, is now open for tours every Saturday from the beginning of May to the end of September. The exterior of the mansion was restored in the mid-1960s and in 2008 the building underwent further interior and exterior restoration.

Atsion recreational center (photo by Rob Auermuller)

142

Batsto Village

The current scene at Atsion, with its legions of summer bathers, picnickers, and campers, would surely be an incomprehensible sight to those hearty villagers who once labored long hours here with little time for leisure. Though their contribution toward building a new nation is often overlooked, there is a debt we owe them; preserving this unique and historically significant site is certainly the least we can do.

Batsto Village Today

A visit to Batsto Village today, with its significant early American history and bountiful natural attributes, is a many-layered experience. Nestled in the pine forests of southern New Jersey, this open-air museum stretches over 40 acres and consists of 33 historic buildings and structures. A stroll through Batsto's streets offers visitors the opportunity to experience firsthand an earlier time and a different way of life. In addition to being an historical treasure trove, Batsto offers opportunities to encounter and learn about the unique and multifaceted ecosystem of the Pinelands region.

Batsto Village is a New Jersey historic site. It is administered by the New Jersey Department of Environmental Protection's Division of Parks and Forestry, whose mission for the site is three-fold: 1) to preserve, restore, reconstruct, and interpret Batsto's period of historical significance (1766–1954); 2) to teach the history of southern New Jersey; and, 3) to provide visitors with hospitality, service, and products of quality.

A good place to start your Batsto adventure is at the visitor center. The center was renovated and expanded in 2005 to include a museum and a 100-seat auditorium. First-time visitors can view a 10-minute orientation film that will introduce them to the history of the site as well as to the natural resources that first drew people here 250 years ago. The museum houses exhibits that further describe the historical growth of Batsto and the natural aspects of the region.

Tickets for Batsto mansion tours can be purchased at the visitor center and are well worth the nominal fee. In 2008 the mansion underwent a $3.9 million restoration to improve its structural stability

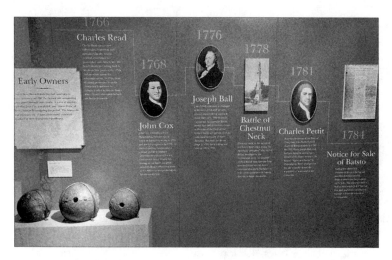

Batsto Museum (photo by Albert D. Horner)

and upgrade the heating, air conditioning, ventilation, fire safety, and security systems. The interior was also restored to return the mansion to its 1880s appearance. In-depth tours are conducted by knowledgeable guides, who provide visitors with information about the mansion's construction and furnishings and share stories about the families who resided there. Fifteen of the mansion's 36 rooms are open to the public on these guided tours.

The visitor center features a gift shop where a variety of books on the ecology, culture, and history of the region are available, along with an excellent selection of gifts and souvenirs for adults and children of all ages.

Before leaving the center visitors can pick up a brochure at the information desk to assist with a self-guided walking tour of the village. The site employs multiple methods to interpret the village and enhance the experience for visitors, including a smartphone guided tour. Accompanied by a walking guide checklist, the smartphone tour highlights 18 historic locations throughout the village. Visitors simply scan the QR code at each location along the way. The smartphone audiovisual tour lasts approximately 40 minutes and includes a 2–3 minute presentation at each stop. Wayside exhibits

Gift shop (photo by Albert D. Horner)

throughout the village also enhance the experience for visitors. In addition to the information provided in this chapter, there are special events and tours on the village website at batstovillage.org and maps, videos, and podcasts on the Wharton State Forest website at www.state.nj.us/dep/parksandforests/parks/wharton.html.

On seasonal weekends and during special events, Batsto Village functions as a living history museum where visitors can enjoy live demonstrations by a working blacksmith and view the sawmill in operation. Plans are in the works to provide additional live interpretation of the village, to include demonstrations at the carpenter's shop and gristmill.

The Batsto Post Office is interpreted by staff and volunteers on seasonal Saturdays and during special events. The company store, set up to reflect its 19th-century appearance, is open daily to visitors and includes interpretive displays.

Seasonal events include the well-attended autumn Country Living Fair; the Antique and Bottle Show; and Winter Holiday and Halloween celebrations. Past historically-themed Second Saturday programs have included Revolutionary and Civil War encampments

Blacksmiths Toby and Kate Kroll (photo by Albert D. Horner)

and reenactments, classic car shows, art festivals, and glassblowing demonstrations.

A full-time naturalist presides over a variety of weekly activities including wildlife programs, guided nature walks, and canoe tours around Batsto Lake. The Annie M. Carter Nature Center houses exhibits on the flora and fauna of the region including live animal exhibits. The story of the Jersey Devil and other local legends and ghost stories are featured in fall programs, which also include a twilight woods walk.

Evening astronomy and "star watch" programs are offered in the spring, summer, and fall. Participants have the opportunity to look through a variety of telescopes at planets, star clusters, and galaxies and to learn about the constellations. The astronomy and star watch programs are offered by a local astronomy club. A schedule of special events is available at the information desk in the visitor center.

Visitors can take a leisurely stroll by the lake and sawmill or pick up a free trail guide at the visitor center and take a more ambitious self-guided hike into the surrounding woodlands. The well-known Batona trail is just one of the marked foot paths that passes through the village. Picnic tables, located at the back of the visitor center parking lot, are available for those interested in enjoying an outdoor meal during their visit. Vending machines offering soft drinks, water, and light snacks are located in front of the visitor center. On seasonal weekends a vendor who sells soft drinks and fast food items can often be found in the visitor center parking lot.

"Batsto Through the Years: A Teaching Resource" is a handbook developed to help educators teach the importance of the New Jersey Pinelands while focusing on the lifestyles of the people who once lived and worked there. The guide's 10 lessons are based on the fourth grade New Jersey Core Curriculum Standards. Topics range from the environment and early Pinelands industries to daily life in the village. The handbook, which is best used in conjunction with a visit to the site, provides orientation and follow-up activities. It can be downloaded at no charge from the Wharton State Forest website.

Today, Batsto Village, located within the federally established 1.1 million acre Pinelands National Reserve, receives protection from the strongest land use law in the United States. This bodes well for the village, and the future appears bright not only for the survival of this important historic site but also for the preservation of the unique natural environment that surrounds it.

Bibliography

"Batsto Village Plan." NJ Department of Environmental Protection and Energy, Division of Parks and Forestry, December 1993.

"Batsto Was Warned of Coming Attack." *Batsto Citizens Gazette*, Summer/Winter 1982.

Bernstein, Herbert. "Batsto—The Oldest Operating Post Office in the Nation." *Batsto Citizens Gazette*, Spring/Summer 1984.

Bernstein, Herbert. "Hard Times Assailed Batsto But Richards Met Test." *Batsto Citizens Gazette*, Spring/Summer 1980.

Boyer, Charles S. *Early Forges and Furnaces in New Jersey.* Philadelphia: University of Pennsylvania Press, 1931.

Boucher, Jack; Atlantic City Historical Society. *Absegami Yesteryear.* Egg Harbor City, NJ: Laureate Press, 1963.

Boucher, Jack. *Of Batsto and Bog Iron.* Batsto, NJ: Batsto Citizens Committee, 1964.

Brumbaugh, G. Edwin. Historical Aspects of the Wharton Tract: Atlantic, Burlington, Camden Counties New Jersey: Report. NJ: s.n., 1960.

Buck, Watson. "A Day With the Old Iron Makers at Batsto." *Batsto Citizens Gazette*, March 1966.

"Chestnut Neck Stops Batsto Bound British." *Batsto Citizens Gazette*, Summer/Fall 1984.

Cresson, Jack. "Batsto Mansion Story Shrouded By Time—Archaeological Committee Seeks Data." *Batsto Citizens Gazette*, Spring/Summer 1987.

Cresson, Jack. "Hydraulic Ram at Batsto: Another View of the Past." *Batsto Citizens Gazette*, Spring/Summer 1994.

Cresson, Jack. "Prehistory and Batsto's Environs." *Batsto Citizens Gazette*, Fall/Winter 1996.

Cresson, Jack. "A Short History of Archaeological Research of Batsto and Its Environs." *Batsto Citizens Gazette*, Winter/Spring 1996.

Dellomo, Angelo N. Jr. "Elias Wright Put Together Wharton's Pineland Empire." *Batsto Citizens Gazette*, Summer/Winter 1982.

Eckhardt, Gertrude. "Family of Wm. Richards 'Home' to Batsto." *Batsto Citizens Gazette*, Summer/Fall 1984.

Ewing, Sarah W. R. 1979. *Atsion: A Town of Four Faces*. Batsto, NJ: Batsto Citizens Committee, 1979.

Ewing, Sarah W. R. "Barons Made Fortune At Batsto Long Ago." Batsto Citizens Committee, Spring/Summer 1978.

Ewing, Sarah W. R. "The Batsto Citizen's Committee: How It Was in 1989." *Batsto Citizens Gazette*, Fall/Winter 1995.

Ewing, Sarah W. R. *Batsto Lights: The Story of Batsto Glass and the Richards Dynasty*. Batsto, NJ: Batsto Citizens Committee, 1979.

Ewing, Sarah W. R. "Commentary Regarding Batsto Plan." *Batsto Citizens Gazette*, Spring/Summer 1994.

Ewing, Sarah W. R. "Daily Life in Batsto Village is Described." *Batsto Citizens Gazette*, Summer/Fall 1978.

Ewing, Sarah W. R. "How the Batsto Mansion Came to Be Furnished." *Batsto Citizens Gazette*, Spring/Summer 1981.

Ewing, Sarah W. R. *An Introduction to Batsto*. Batsto, NJ: Batsto Citizens Committee, 1986.

Ewing, Sarah W. R. "Joseph Wharton Descendants Gather." *Batsto Citizens Gazette*, Fall/Winter 1980.

Ewing, Sarah W. R. "Samuel Richards Mansion Unchanged Through the Years." *Batsto Citizens Gazette*, Spring/Summer 1979.

Flemming, George. "Indians' Atsion Role Disputed By Writer." *Batsto Citizens Gazette*, Fall/Winter 1979.

Gowaskie, Joseph. *Workers in New Jersey History*. Trenton, NJ: New Jersey Historical Commission, Department of State, 1996.

Greene, Pettit. "Letters Shed Light on Batsto." *Batsto Citizens Gazette*, Spring/Summer 1983.

Griffith, Robert. "Excavation at Batsto Unearths Hydraulic Ram." *Batsto Citizens Gazette*, Winter/Spring 1982.

Griffith, Robert. "Joseph Wharton: 'Iron Man' of New Jersey." *Batsto Citizens Gazette*, Winter/Fall 1986.

Hawke, Judith. *Everyday Life in Early America*. New York: Harper & Row, 1988.

"Hidden Room in Mansion Gave Rise to Fanciful Legend." *Batsto Citizen Gazette*, Fall/Winter 1978.

Karnoutsos, Carmela Ascolese. *New Jersey Women: A History of Their Status, Roles and Images*. Trenton NJ: New Jersey Historical Commission, Department of State, 1997.

Kemp, Franklin W. *A Nest of Rebel Pirates*. Batsto, NJ: Batsto Citizens Committee, 1966.

"Key Found to Tunnel Under the Batsto Mansion." *Batsto Citizens Gazette*, Summer/Fall 1988.

Kier, C. F. Jr. "Batsto Village to Host Wharton Family Homecoming." *Batsto Citizens Gazette*, Summer/Fall 1980.

Kier, C. F. Jr. "It's Business As Usual During Construction." *Batsto Citizens Gazette*, Winter/Spring 1982.

Kier, Charles. "Richards Family Will Gather At Batsto." *Batsto Citizens Gazette*, Winter/Spring 1984.

Kirby, Lois Ann. "Changes/Additions to the Plan." *Batsto Citizens Gazette*, Fall/Winter 1996.

Kirby, Lois Ann. "It's Business as Usual During Construction." *Batsto Citizens Gazette*, Winter/Spring 1982.

Kirby, Lois Ann. "William Richards' Later Life." *Batsto Citizens Gazette*, Fall/Winter 1993.

Kirby & Van Istendal. "Update of the Batsto Controversy." *Batsto Citizens Gazette*, Fall/Winter 1995.

Koedel, R. Craig. "Mullica River Ships in the Age of Sail." *Batsto Citizens Gazette*, Summer/Fall 1987.

Lewis, W. David and Walter Hugins. *Hopewell Furnace: A Guide to Hopewell Village National Historic Site, Pennsylvania.* Washington, DC: U.S. Department of the Interior, 1983.

Lippincott, Bertram. *An Historical Sketch of Batsto New Jersey.* Batsto, NJ: Batsto Citizens Committee, 1933.

Martyniuk, Carol A. "Batsto Mansion Shrouded By Time—Earliest Building Unknown." *Batsto Citizens Gazette*, Spring/Summer 1987.

Pearce, John E. *Heart of the Pines: Ghostly Voices of the Pine Barrens.* Hammonton, NJ: Batsto Citizens Committee, 2000.

Pepper, Adeline. *The Glass Gaffers of New Jersey.* New York: Charles Scribner's & Sons, 1971.

Pierce, Arthur D. *Family Empire in Jersey Iron: The Richards Enterprises in the Pine Barrens.* New Brunswick, NJ: Rutgers University Press, 1964.

Pierce, Arthur D. *Iron in the Pines: The Story of New Jersey's Ghost Towns and Bog Iron.* New Brunswick, NJ: Rutgers University Press, 1957.

Pierce, Arthur D. *Smugglers Woods: Jaunts and Journeys in Colonial and Revolutionary New Jersey.* New Brunswick, NJ: Rutgers University Press, 1960.

"Privateers and Mariners in the Revolutionary War." American Merchant Marine at War. www.usmm.org/revolution.html.

Solem-Stull, Barbara. *The Forks: A Brief History of the Area.* Medford, NJ: Plexus Publishing, Inc., 2002.

Solem-Stull, Barbara. *Ghost Towns and Other Quirky Places in the New Jersey Pine Barrens.* Medford, NJ: Plexus Publishing, Inc., 2005.

Weaver, Beverly A. "Balancing the Scales in the Batsto Village Controversy." *Batsto Citizens Gazette*, Spring/Summer 1995.

Weaver, Beverly A. "Batsto: A Restful Haven Amidst the Pines." *Batsto Citizens Gazette*, Fall/Winter 1977

Weaver, Beverly A. "George Washington: The Legend, The Man, The Icon." *Batsto Citizens Gazette*, Winter/Spring 1994.

Weaver, Beverly A. "Joseph Wharton: Pioneering With Forest Management, Part I." *Batsto Citizens Gazette*, Spring/Summer 1991.

Weaver, Beverly A. "Joseph Wharton: Pioneering With Forest Management Part II." *Batsto Citizens Gazette*, Summer/Fall 1991.

Wharton, Hollingsworth, Anne. *Salons Colonial and Republican.* Philadelphia: J. B. Lippincott Company, 1900.

Wilson, Budd. "The 1993 Batsto Village Plan." *Batsto Citizens Gazette*, Spring/Summer 1995.

Wilson, Budd. "Batsto Village: Countdown to Restoration." *Batsto Citizens Gazette*, Summer/Fall 1996.

Wilson, Budd. "Batsto Village: Roads and Streets." *Batsto Citizens Gazette*, Winter/Spring 1996.

Wilson, Budd. "Batsto Village: The Last Days." *Batsto Citizens Gazette*, Summer/Fall 1995.

Wilson, Budd. "Batsto Village: Types of Workers Housing." *Batsto Citizens Gazette*, Spring/Summer 1996.

Wilson, Budd. "Batsto Visitor Center Permanent Exhibit." *Batsto Citizens Gazette*, Fall/Winter 1983.

Wilson, Budd. "In Defense of a Dead Man." *Batsto Citizens Gazette*, Fall/Winter 1994.

Wilson, J. G. "Fire Ravaged Batsto Back in Year of 1874." *Batsto Citizens Gazette*, Spring/Summer 1978.

Wilson, J. G. "General Wright Key to Assembling Wharton's Holdings." *Batsto Citizens Gazette*, Spring/Summer 1981.

Wilson, J. G. "General Wright Was Architect of the Wharton Forest." *Batsto Citizens Gazette*, Winter/Spring 1984.

Wilson, J. G. "Joseph Wharton: Man of Vision and Enterprise." *Batsto Citizens Gazette*, Spring/Summer 1978.

Wilson, J. G. "Legends Clinging to Batsto Show No Signs of Giving Up." *Batsto Citizens Gazette*, Spring/Summer 1980.

Wilson, J. G. "Sugar Making Experiment Conducted By Wharton." *Batsto Citizens Gazette*, Summer/Fall 1984.

Winsch, C. E. "State Plan for Batsto Creates Controversy." *Batsto Citizens Gazette*, Spring/Summer 1994.

"Work on Expanded Visitor Center at Batsto Starts." *Batsto Citizens Gazette*, Fall/Winter 1981.

Yates, W. Ross. *Joseph Wharton: Quaker Industrial Pioneer.* Cranberry, NJ: Associated University Presses, 1987.

Vail, George C. "Little Church of the Pines." *Batsto Citizens Gazette*, Winter/Spring 1991.

About the Author and Photographer

Author **Barbara Solem** has an undergraduate degree in psychology from the College of New Jersey (formerly Trenton State College). She has completed graduate work in education administration and has been a special education teacher, a trainer, a principal, and an administrator. Barbara retired from the State of New Jersey Department of Human Services, Office of Education, in 2002, having worked as an education administrator for 15 years.

A popular Pine Barrens speaker and resident of Shamong, New Jersey, Barbara is the author of two previous Plexus books: *The Forks: A Brief History of the Area* and *Ghost Towns and Other Quirky Places in the New Jersey Pine Barrens*. She is a member of the Batsto Citizens Committee, Inc. and a tour guide at the Atsion Mansion.

Please write Barbara at barbsolem@aol.com.

Albert D. Horner, who contributed his photographic talents to *Batsto Village*, is a resident of Medford Lakes, New Jersey. A self-taught photographer since the late 1970s, Al currently spends his time capturing intimate landscapes of his favorite subject, the New Jersey Pine Barrens.

Al's work is frequently exhibited in local galleries, and he conducts photography workshops and gives talks based on his images as well as his knowledge of the local environment. He believes that, "Although the Pinelands does not have mountain peaks or lush valleys with babbling brooks, it has a beauty and uniqueness all its own." It is his greatest ambition "to capture the beauty of the Pine Barrens and then have those images help preserve it."

Many of Al's photos may be viewed at www.pinelandsimagery.com.

155

Index